In Search of the Church
Keys From the Journey

Douglas A. Hagey

xulon PRESS

Copyright © 2007 by Douglas A. Hagey

In Search of the Church
Keys From the Journey
by Douglas A. Hagey

Printed in the United States of America

ISBN 978-1-60477-143-5

All rights reserved solely by the author. The author guarantees all contents are original and do not infringe upon the legal rights of any other person or work. No part of this book may be reproduced in any form without the permission of the author. The views expressed in this book are not necessarily those of the publisher.

Unless otherwise indicated, Bible quotations are taken from the New American Standard Bible, version of the Bible, Copyright 1960, 1962, 1963, 1968, 1971, 1972, 1973, 1975, 1977 by The Lockman Foundation, and the New International Version, version of the Bible, Copyright 1973, 1978, 1984 by International Bible Society, and the The Message, version of the Bible, Copyright 1993, 1994, 1995 by NavPress Publishing Group.

www.xulonpress.com

Acknowledgements

Ellie is my friend, lover, roommate, mother of our three wonderful daughters, and my wife too! I cannot imagine life without her. This book is her story too because we are one.

Tonya, Rachel and Sarah are three sources of the greatest pride in my life. They lived much of this journey with me and still love me. They have helped to stretch me to think outside of prescribed boxes and have made fatherhood a joyful thing for me. They are really special!

My mother and father provided a Christian context for me to begin my journey and now cheer from the stands, hoping that I will finish well.

Howard, Paulette, Barry, Esther and Evelyn began their journeys around the same time I did, and have taught me many things that only brothers and sisters can.

Uncle Eric Davey and Joe Opperman taught me by their lives that service is more important than position, that being authentically yourself is being like Jesus.

My Wellspring Family in Dinuba (and beyond) allowed me the freedom to try to fly on my own, without trying to clip my wings or focus on my failures. Their lifelong friendships are proof of the mystery of the gospel.

My Gleanings for the Hungry Family has supported and blessed me in my journey and has reminded me of my call to love the poor. My friendship with Wally and Norma has been a highlight of my life.

My Northern BC Family has often reminded me of the beauty and diversity that makes up the church. Their sincere friendship has been so appreciated.

My Emerge Family has personified unconditional love to me and others. Some of my *conclusions* about the church were solidified in our living room and at Ethical Addictions Café as we shared our lives together in openness and sincerity. Thanks especially to Nicole, Sandra, Jen, Bubba, Pierre and Andrew who were the first to embrace new ways of thinking about being church, and who helped give me a reason to hope that church could be *fun* again. Special thanks to Sandra for lovingly editing my manuscript.

My Foursquare Canada Family is as diverse as the country itself. They loved me even though I didn't fit into fixed categories. Special thanks to Les and Anita who have taught me much about life and death, and to Steve and Mike who are my great friends.

My Pacific Life Bible College students have challenged me to a deeper devotion to loving the church. Their hunger to learn and grow has kept my soul alive and my heart young.

My Vineyard Community Church Family in Shoreline and especially Rich and Rose are helping me to rest in who I really am and enjoy *abundant* life. Thanks for helping me to spread my tired wings and fly again!

Special thanks to my many friends whose friendship surpasses any common membership other than the *Family of God!*

Contents

Introduction – What is the church? ix
Preface – The Journey xv

PART ONE: Let's Take A Trip! 19

1. About the Other Cheek! 21
2. Mothers & Fathers 27
3. There's a Train 'a Coming! 37
4. Calling 41
5. Information or Formation? 47
6. Jesus People 53
7. Tent Tea 61
8. Saturday Night Live and Beyond 69
9. The Wellspring Experiment 73

PART TWO: Are We There Yet, Dad? 89

10. Family Ties 91
11. Survival 95
12. Death and Dying 99
13. Burnout 119
14. Renewal: Expired Shelf-Life 125

15. Return to Hockey-land 129

PART THREE: Is This the Destination? 139

16. Cowboys and Indians 141
17. Farmers and Funerals 145
18. Gender Gap 149
19. What Did Jesus Say? 157
20. Prototype 167

PART FOUR: Next Rest Stop 50 Miles! 205

21. On the Road Again! 207

Introduction: What Is The Church?

*I worship the God of our fathers
as a follower of the Way.*
Acts 24:14 NIV

My life is wonderfully enhanced when one of my sweet grandchildren sends me an artful crayon *masterpiece*. "And what is this over here, Jonah?" I ask my little grandson, needing an interpretation of his art. "Papa! It's a dog!!" He replies, with disbelief in his voice that anyone could have missed the clarity of definition with which he has created these two circles and four sticks. Of course… a dog!

How would you describe a dog to me? Before you begin, tell me what picture you have in your mind. How generic is your picture? It is almost impossible to describe what a dog is (dogginess) without actually picturing some kind of a dog (German Shepherd, Collie, Poodle, etc). Having just parted with a wonderfully rambunctious male Golden Retriever, whom I affectionately named "Moose" for his clumsiness and knack of always being in my way, I picture him when asked to describe a dog. The same difficulty arises when trying to define other things as well. What is a friend? (I see Steve and Mike and Barry and Les). What is food? (cheesecake and moose-burgers). What is church? (Remember the little game we played as kids with our fingers intertwined: Here's the church and here's the steeple... open the church and here's the people). How can I discover what the church is truly meant to be when I carry so many pictures in my mind from my experiences with a variety of expressions of the church. What is the church?

Perhaps going back to the *original* will help. In Acts 2 we read a very simple, yet deeply insightful description of the earliest church. It is important to remember that the gathered saints (Jewish converts) had historical patterns for ways of meeting and being *religious.* Temple worship was the common practice for these first believers. It should not surprise us that they continued "in the temple" because it was their custom. If they had been asked to describe church they would likely have used some historical definitions for the way they gathered. "Ekklesia" was a gathering or assembly of the people. But, they would have also described an unfolding picture of the new thing that was springing up around them. As they met together after Pentecost, there was a deep, personal commitment to each other, the sharing of possessions with all in need, and daily gatherings in homes to fellowship, pray, break bread and grow in their faith. <u>These things were not simply copies from a previous religious experience, but were the new, real, dynamic and spontaneous expressions</u> of transformed minds and hearts. If these practices were not merely copied from previous experience, where did they come from?

The most likely answer is embedded in the name by which these saints were called. <u>These "Followers of The Way"</u> patterned their decisions after the teachings of their leader. Jesus had taught them to love one another, to forgive, to care for those in need, to be at peace with one another.

They were living out these truths in practical expressions of faith. There was a beautiful simplicity to their lives and to their meetings. The early church leaders expanded on the "one another" commands from the Master as they wrote:

> *Be devoted to one another in brotherly love. (Romans 12:10)*
> *Give preference to one another in honor. (Romans 12:10)*
> *Be of the same mind toward one another. (Romans 12:16)*
> *Accept one another just as Christ also accepted us. (Romans 15:7)*
> *Admonish one another. (Romans 15:14)*
> *Through love serve one another. (Galatians 5:13)*
> *Show forbearance to one another in love. (Ephesians 4:2)*
> *Be kind to one another. (Ephesians 4:32)*
> *Do not lie to one another. (Colossians 3:9)*
> *Comfort one another. (1 Thessalonians 4:18)*
> *Encourage one another. (1 Thessalonians 5:11)*
> *Build up one another. (1 Thessalonians 5:11)*
> *Live in peace with one another. (1 Thessalonians 5:13)*
> *Always seek after that which is good for one another. (1 Thessalonians 5:15)*
> *Let us consider how to stimulate one another to love and good deeds. (Hebrews 10:24)*
> *Do not speak against one another. (James 4:11)*
> *Confess your sins to one another. (James 5:16)*
> *Pray for one another. (James 5:16)*
> *Keep fervent in your love for one another. (1 Peter 4:8)*
> *Be hospitable to one another without complaint. (1 Peter 4:9)*

> *Clothe yourself with humility toward one another. (1 Peter 5:5)*

It is clear that these early followers focused their energies on the development of relationships rather than the building of institutions. Being filled with the spirit of Christ, they lived out His teachings.

Ever since my early Bible College days I have been asking this question, *"What is the church?"* My journey has led me through a labyrinth of discovery. My dear friend Mike recently informed me that the answer to that question is quite simple. Knowing that I was writing a whole book on the subject, he said with a twinkle in his eye, "It is the people of God". Of course he is right, but it has still been my lifelong passion to know what Jesus had in mind for His people when He said "I will build My church." As I have been writing I have been aware of the distinction usually placed on the church as local church and universal *Church*. I do not attempt to differentiate in this manner; but simply refer to the church (lower case) as followers of Jesus learning and growing together in faith and mission regardless of their location or time in history.

This book is not about deconstructing the church and leaving it disemboweled on the operating table. I love the church! I do not love everything that we have done to the church, or everything that we have done in the name of church, but **I love the church!** Sometimes surgery is necessary to restore health. Surgery is painful, recovery is often slow, but the alternative of a lifetime of carrying the pain of a debilitating disease that inhibits our ability to fulfill our destiny is senseless.

The desire of my heart is to be honest in diagnosing the church without becoming a cynic, to cut into the church and expose the sources of pain without denying my own involvement in causing that pain, to participate in the healing process without suggesting that I am alone or have all the answers. It is my hope and prayer that you will join me on my journey *"In Search of the Church."*

Preface: The Journey

*I will instruct you and teach you
in the way which you should go;*
Ps 32:8 NASB

It had been a great house for Ellie and me, a peaceful place, home for seven years. The last couple of years were quite earth shaking as the street was widened to four lanes, and our beautiful hedge, the only barrier between us and the busy traffic, had been ripped out and replaced with junior cedars, a meager excuse for a barrier. Progress is usually only understood and appreciated by those who directly benefit from what the rest of us perceive as turmoil. We lived for those two years under the monthly anxiety of receiving a two-month notice to vacate from the developers. The day finally came. We had until the end of January 2007 to pack up and be gone.

As I sat in my office toward the end of our time there, my attention was drawn to a huge ring of keys on my bookshelf. Over the years I had collected keys that I no longer needed, or simply couldn't remember what lock they fit. We had ministered in various places, we had keys to church buildings and had been given keys to people's houses and garages and padlocks. There was a key and remote for a car that had been totaled in an accident. Old dog tags reminded me of the faithfulness of Lassie and Canuck, both having completed their long years of service.

Most of us have spare keys in the bottom of our catch-all drawer. I have this gnawing concern that if I throw them away, I will someday have a moment of healed memories and realize what they unlock. Between Ellie and me, we have accumulated quite an impressive collection. These keys had unlocked our lives, but were now just objects on a ring.

Isn't it amazing how God can take simple objects in our lives and spin them into a web of discovery and insight? I began to see that the keys represented many stopping places on our journey. Their stories were linked with the people, places and events that had filled our moments and days. Some of them were shrouded in pain and sorrow, others clouded with doubt and disappointment. Others were from the times of great joy that had accompanied the birth of our three wonderful daughters. These were not simply metal objects that had served their purpose and now needed to be destroyed. They were the **keys from the journey.**

Ellie and I find such joy in hearing the stories of people around us. How often we have sat in church meetings wondering what is going through the minds and hearts of the people sitting near us. What are their hopes and dreams? How did they get to this point in their lives? What pain are they sheltering in their souls that few others know about? What brings joy to their hearts? What are the unanswered questions that drift through their minds? What is their story?

My Christian roots have taught me that the journey is mostly about the destination. My Baby Boomer membership has reinforced that idea with its own definitions of success and achievement. However, after years of hearing the stories of others and reviewing our own passage through life, we have begun to see the journey as the destination. Of course we still believe in eternity, in heaven and in a future lived out in some other amazing dimension that is beyond our present ability to comprehend. But, we are aware of the tragedy of missing the meaning of the journey by only focusing on its ending.

I have often been the object of laughter on a road trip, when I have constantly pointed out a myriad of finer details that others might have missed. "Did you see that eagle on the post? Look at the moose running into the woods! That license plate bracket said, 'If you can read this you are too damn close'. Look at those mountains! Look at that valley! Did you see that tarantula spider crossing the road?" By their reaction, I have discerned that not everyone who rides with me is as focused as I am on the details of the trip. Some simply want to know "When will we be there?"

I do not want to miss the beauty and meaning of the next step by looking too far beyond it. The hidden treasures are along the pathway, but will be missed and lost unless I learn to look with different eyes.

As I relate my story to you I will point out some of what I have seen along the way. I will introduce you to some of the people of the journey, some of the places and events. I will share the insights that are my keys from the journey. I invite you into my story. My hope is that it will encourage you to revisit your own.

PART ONE: Let's Take A Trip!

*Anticipation is often greater than realization...
but "doing" has rewards
that "thinking about doing" does not!
DH*

*It may be hard for an egg to turn into a bird.
It would be a jolly sight harder for it
to learn to fly while remaining an egg.
We are like eggs at present,
and you cannot go on indefinitely
being just an ordinary, decent egg.
We must be hatched or go bad.
C. S. Lewis*

*Faith is taking the first step
even when you don't see
the whole staircase.
Martin Luther King, Jr.*

ONE:

About The Other Cheek!

Whoever hits you on the cheek,
offer him the other also.
Luke 6:29 NASB

How much of what is presented in church as truth,
can be applied in the marketplace of our lives?
DH

My parents, especially my mother, taught us as young boys the value, importance and divinely decreed command to be non-combatants. We knew that if a fight arose with any of the pugnacious neighborhood boys, even over such important life issues as a dirty hit in street hockey, that we were required by our *religion* to take whatever they threw our way, and then "turn the other cheek", whatever that meant. As I recall there was ample opportunity for us to live out our religious conviction in our rather rough neighborhood.

Then it all crashed around me! It was recess time at Paris Central School. A fresh, wet snowfall welcomed us to the playground. Without warning I was thrown to the ground, had my arms pinned and my face washed in cold, wet snow. Looking up through slushy eyes I could see the perpetrator of this cowardly attack. It was Bobby the Bully, feared by all the boys at Central.

I can only tell you that at that moment something stirred deeply within my soul. My heart was racing, my mind repeating the maternal mantra about my cheeks, my emotions raging with feelings that I had not fully explored before. "I can't take this anymore... I won't take this anymore!" In that brief moment I evaluated my total existence, my destiny, my religious belief system and my reputation with all the other boys who were surrounding this snow-covered heap with shouts of encouragement for Bobby to do more than he had done. I can only assume that their shouts for more were simply a protective mechanism to keep Bobby busy with me and not bullying them.

In an instant I made a desperate decision. Even if it meant that I would go to "H-E-double hockey sticks" (I was not permitted to say *Hell* straight up in those days), I was not about to turn any cheek of mine. Having made this eternal decision, I sprang into action. I threw Bobby off of me and onto a fresh patch of snow, pinned him down and washed his face with ice-cold, wet snow.

Oh! What a feeling! It was the exhilaration of being in control. It was the thrill of hearing the supportive shouts of little boys cheering my manhood and suggesting mean things that I might consider doing to this bully. Looking deeply into Bobby's eyes I said, "Don't ever do that to me again!" With shocked disbelief etched upon his face he responded with a quivering promise to never bully me again. He became one of my best friends and treated my growing circle of friends with the same respect.

This was perhaps the first time that I experienced a real-life, out-in-the-world situation that required me to <u>consider a practical application of my beliefs</u>. I concluded that I had sinned, fallen short of my parent's beliefs, exposed myself to the anger of a God I didn't really know. I anxiously awaited the next altar call at church so I could rid myself of the weight of this awful sin.

Years later I recognized that moment as one of early leadership, of concern for justice, of standing alone regardless of the outcome. I had joined John Eldredge's **Wild At Heart**. He said it well when he wrote:

Don't ask yourself what the world needs. Ask yourself what makes you come alive, and go do that, because what the world needs, is people who have come alive! (2001, Thomas Nelson Publishers, Nashville, TN)

That day at recess I had strangely "come alive"!

Last summer I was spending the evening with my grandchildren in California so that Ellie, Jesse and Rachel could go out for a movie. I had fed the three of them and was cleaning up when I heard this conversation between Jonah (5) who was holding his favorite action figure and Haley (7):

Jonah: "Hello little girl, and how are you? Where's your mom and dad?"
Haley: "Oh! My mom and dad died in a terrible car accident."
Jonah: "Well, I can climb up to heaven with this string and get them back for you!"
Haley (hands on hips looking indignant): "The Lord Jesus says in chapter *something* that you can't get into heaven with a string."

I was bent over the sink in laughter when I realized that Haley had heard many chapel speakers at her Christian school preaching to her in a way that was similar to how she had just rebuffed little Jonah's attempt to be helpful. I wondered again just how much of what we are taught in a Christian context translates into real life situations?

Church should be a place to grow in authentic faith, with people who are transparently real with each other in every relationship of their lives. We should be able to openly discuss the issues of our lives in light of what we believe to be true from scripture. A young boy should be able to tell his recess story and find comfort among the friends of Jesus who will not sentence him to Hell. We may not all agree on the meaning and application of truth, but unconditional love accepts those whose lives and beliefs do not mimic our own. It embraces all people because we are all made in His image. It is the most authentic expression of our own changed hearts.

An example of an attempt by a church to apply taught-truth was related to me by my good friends Larry and Judy who participated in a church *experiment* in Colorado Springs. The Sunday morning worship space was set up with round tables and chairs. Coffee and donuts were served. Music was kept to a minimum and was basically a performed song by the band. The talk by the pastor was brief, topical and practical. Table discussion about what it meant and how it could be applied was the main event. This was good for both *saint and sinner* alike. What creative ways can we discover to merge truth with *shoe-leather* in our lives? How can church gatherings become fully supportive of our real life on the outside? How can the whole church participate in the process of discovering and applying truth?

It seems to me that a spiritual leader who recognizes the need for applied truth, will not be slighted or feel diminished by giving up some of her or his platform preaching time for the sake of an exercise in application. This could be done individually by each member, or done in small groups. It is time that we, as leaders, recognize and appreciate the incredible value of the discerning responses of God's people to our sermons.

comfort among friends

TWO:

Mothers and Fathers

*For if you were to have countless tutors in Christ,
yet you would not have many fathers.*
1 Corinthians 4:14 NASB

*What would the church look like
if every spiritual leader
was devoted to reaching out
to emerging leaders
with an authentic desire for their success?*
DH

It was my mother's father, Grampa Davey, who encouraged me to keep coming back to the construction site. I was only fifteen at the time, but wanted a job and Grampa was the custodian for a school that was being enlarged that summer in the little town of Paris, Ontario. Ollie, the foreman, had turned me down, saying there was no opening. Grampa encouraged me to come back every day and keep asking. I didn't know until much later that behind the scene he was promoting me and my virtues to Ollie. After three days of asking, I watched as Ollie assessed the two young boys who were filling a wheelbarrow with bricks in a very slow, unproductive way. After a few minutes he turned to me and said that I should come in at seven on Monday morning. I never saw the other two boys again.

Every day I had lunch with Grampa. Every day I heard encouraging words from his mouth. Because of what I heard, I just knew that I could do anything I put my mind and heart into. That was the pattern of my relationship with him over the next few years that he was with us. His death was the loss of a dear friend, a true mentor.

My mother's brother, Uncle Eric, was raised in the image of Grampa. He had no children of his own, but invested years of his life in his boys' Sunday School class at Evangelistic Center. I remember in vivid detail some of those wonderful classes. He built the walls of Jericho in the middle of that little basement room and had us march around them and shout and scream until they all fell down. Other classes were viewing flat felt images on Flannel graph boards, while we were carried away in our minds and placed in the midst of the story itself. Regularly on Sunday afternoon, Uncle Eric would pick all of us boys up in his car and drive out into the *wild* country. He had this amazing ability to arrive atop a farmer's wooden bridge just before the old steam locomotive and train arrived. We would hear the roaring, feel the shaking, and then be engulfed in the belching smoke and steam of this marvel of engineering. Our shouts and screams brought delight to his eyes. This manly adventure was always followed with peanut butter sandwiches that had been hidden away until that moment.

We all knew that we were loved and special and valuable. The many young boys that he mentored would affirm a hundred times over the virtues of our dear Uncle Eric. Through later years of my life, even after marriage and children, he would still find ways to encourage me in my journey. So often, when I was coloring outside the lines in ministry, he would tell me that he had always known that I would not do the ordinary.

When his earthly voice was silenced by eternity recently, I lost a friend, a father, a model of spiritual fruit, a true lifelong mentor. The tribute that I wrote for his memorial service sheds light on the value of his investment in my life as a young man:

> *As I have reflected upon the depth of character and breadth of Godly influence of this precious man, I have concluded that it was his Christ-likeness that so deeply touched and affected our lives. Perhaps the best description of Uncle Eric is the Fruit of the Spirit listed by the Apostle Paul in the Book of Galatians.*
>
> *<u>LOVE</u>:*
> *Jesus said that the greatest commandment was to love the Lord with all our heart, soul, mind and strength and then love our neighbor as ourselves. Uncle Eric lived a life of consistent fulfillment of both of these commandments. If your life was intersected by his, you knew that he loved the Lord with everything that was within him, and you were the recipient of his warm, neighborly love.*
>
> *<u>JOY</u>:*
> *Oh! That wonderful, joyful smile that he lavished upon all of us. I never doubted his approval or enthusiastic support for my projects and ministry endeavors, for upon his face was written the joy-filled response to my every word. That twinkle in his eye and that incredible smile... Oh! How often he affirmed me and encouraged me to continue my pursuits.*

PEACE:
In Romans 12:18 it says, "If possible, so far as it depends on you, be at peace with all men." Uncle Eric was a man whose heart was ruled by peace. Because he was filled with peace, he became a "peacemaker." "Blessed are the peacemakers, for they shall be called the sons of God."

PATIENCE:
What kind of man would devote year after year to a small Sunday School class of young, unruly boys in the basement of the old Evangelistic Centre? His patient, nurturing care modeled something so deep and profound that us grown-up "little boys" bear the imprint that he quietly and patiently stamped upon our young hearts and minds. I have always believed that God can break down any obstacle that hinders my life and ministry... due in great part to the little cardboard Jericho walls that Uncle Eric erected on the floor of that little classroom... that came tumbling down as we ran and shouted around them. I join the Rick Goodbrands, Howard and Barry Hageys, Barry Hamiltons, Reid Etheringtons and multiplied others of this world... with a heart of indebted gratitude for his patient investment into our young lives.

KINDNESS:
I so clearly recall the personal sense of ownership that filled my heart when I informed the boys' class that even though everyone called him "Uncle" Eric... he was indeed "My Uncle" Eric. I had a special inside track... my mom was his sister... Didn't they get it? He was my "Real Uncle." I was not willing to share all of him with the rest of the boys. But, Uncle Eric

nonetheless continued to reach out in kindness to all of us.

GOODNESS:
Oh! How well do I remember those wonderful Sunday afternoon trips. He would pick up all of the boys in his car, take us for a ride down adventurous, dirt roads into the country... then suddenly he would turn down a lane, climb an old, steep, wooden farmer's railway crossing and park on top. Within seconds we would hear it! As the old steam engine approached we shouted with fearful excitement, the bridge shook, the car shook, we all shook as we were engulfed in billows of black smoke. It didn't get much more exciting than that for us little, Paris boys. Always, a box of peanut butter sandwiches was brought forward to celebrate another successful adventure. How did he always know when and where that train would be? I have continued to love old trains to this day... reminders of those treasured moments with a man so full of goodness.

FAITHFULNESS:
Our God is a Faithful God, and Uncle Eric was a man who walked in Godly faithfulness. A description of him would be the church member of any pastor's dreams. He was committed to Auntie Eva, to his church family, to all of us. He was faithful in all his ways, a man of integrity, faithful in character, a man of his word.

GENTLENESS:
It has been said that "still waters run deep." There was a calm, gentle spirit upon this man. Perhaps being the only boy in a family of girls helped to develop this

gentleness. I am told of the time he discovered his little, mischievous twin sisters, calling down to him from their perch on the peak of that Saskatchewan barn roof... I am grateful for his calmness and gentleness at that moment, or I might never have existed. He was always a "gentle-man".

SELF-CONTROL:
I have heard the stories of bygone days, of long, intense board meetings filled with lively disagreements, in which Uncle Eric sat in observation with a mind and heart made quiet by the presence of his Master. But, when the time was right, he spoke the words of wisdom, words of understanding that instantly brought clarity, dispelled confusion and restored peace.

THANKYOU, Dear Uncle Eric, for investing in my life, for believing in me as a young man, when I didn't fit the patterns and molds that others followed, but chose to walk paths less-traveled in ministry...

THANKYOU for your Christ-like example that has motivated me to follow you... even as you have followed Christ.

When we moved to California in 1972, I worked with a dear pastor, Joe Opperman. Joe had planted the church and at that time was its only pastor for some twenty-eight years. My intent in coming to his church was to begin climbing the ladder of success in youth ministry within that denomination. He modeled faithfulness, his beautifully simple devotion to Christ and to people was overwhelming. He fathered me, loved me, and made room for me in his life and ministry. My view of ministry and success were transformed over those two years that we spent together. Most of what I learned was not from his words, but from watching his life.

Young women and men desperately need spiritual parents involved in their lives who believe in them. Our view of ourselves is molded by the reflection that we see in the eyes and hearts of those that we esteem to be wiser and more 'traveled' than ourselves. Mentors are not the same as disciplers who share growth information to assist us in our walk of faith. Mentors ask us questions like, "What has God placed in your heart that you are passionate about and to which you would choose to devote your life? How can I help you fulfill that destiny?"

Bobb Biehl shares some important ideas in his book **Mentoring** (1996, Broadman & Holman Publishers, Nashville, TN). He says:

> *Mentoring is a lifelong relationship, in which a mentor helps a protégé reach her or his God-given potential. Mentoring is like having an ideal aunt or uncle whom you respect deeply, who loves you at a family level, cares for you at a close friend level, supports you at a sacrificial level, and offers wisdom at a modern Solomon level.[19] At its essence, mentoring is a relationship.[21] Ideally, in a mentoring relationship there is a bonding of hearts.[22] Mentors are those who have gone before us on the mountain of life, but who pause and extend a hand to help us along the way, or who extend a safety line of love and affirmation that may keep us from falling off the mountain. The mentoring relationship is formed when the mentor turns to the protégé and says, 'I love you, I believe in you, I want to help you succeed. I want to make my experience and resources available to help you in any way I can to become all that God wants you to be.'"[26]*

As I was re-reading these quotes for the first time in several years, I felt a strange combination of joy and sorrow in my soul. I have been blessed with some wonderful mentors who have given me a hand up in my ascent up the mountain, but I also served older men in my early years of ministry who had one focus in their minds. They wanted to know what I could bring to the table to further their vision, their goals, their destiny, their ministry. Most of the pain of those years was caused by having to bury my uniqueness, my passion, my calling, my giftedness, and my contribution in the grave of another man's vision. I was certainly grateful for a job in ministry and wanted to serve with a whole heart, but I simply wasn't prepared for the demand to sacrifice myself on the altar of another's success.

In a small town in California, I had worked for months on some innovative ideas for a new Christian School. I had held public meetings, produced and presented slide shows (a long time before PowerPoint). I thought that I had the blessing and release to do this from my senior pastor. Well into this process, he called me into his office to inform me that if there was going to be such a school in this town he would be the one to develop it, not me. He also made it very clear that he wanted people to "know that he had passed this way." I left his office that afternoon with such a deep pain of rejection. Raw flesh hung from my soul. The one to whom I had looked for a hand up had used that hand to push me aside.

After a stint with the Agape Force in East Texas, Ellie and I returned to another small California town. We had felt that God wanted to do something new in that area and we would be pioneering a new kind of church. We shared these ideas with a few friends. I was quickly approached by a local pastor who confided in me that he had plans to leave his church and wanted me to become the next pastor. He had already visited churches in another country that wanted him to come as soon as possible. We were asked to attend his church and were told that the process would unfold in a few weeks. We led in worship and did much of the teaching and vision-casting for the next several months. Feeling the awkwardness of providing much of the leadership without being the leader, I decided to approach him. When I inquired about his proposed timeline, he angrily responded that he had no intention of leaving. He wanted us in his church to further his ministry rather than starting something new that might be competitive. I was dumbfounded! I was in disbelief. I felt deceived. I felt foolish. I was again slapped by the hand that I thought was reaching out to me in love.

As an emerging leader you should be asking this question: Who is in my life helping me discern who I am, not just trying to fit me into an acceptable slot? Who is willing to be transparent about their journey so that I can avoid some of the pitfalls? Parker J. Palmer writes in **Let Your Life Speak – Listening For The Voice Of Vocation** (2000, Jossey-Bass, A Wiley Co., San Francisco, CA 94103):

> *Many young people today journey in the dark, as the young always have, and we elders do them a disservice when we withhold the shadowy parts of our lives.*

I developed a friendship with a young man who was the son of a preacher and the grandson of a preacher. Everyone assumed that he too would follow that pathway, and eventually fill his father's shoes as a national church leader. When I listened to his heart, I heard another story. He had other gifts and passions, a unique journey of his own. His rebellion against being in ministerial training was rooted in the pressure and expectations of well-meaning, yet insensitive elders.

I am grateful that there is a growing awareness of the need for mentoring, but there are so many wonderful emerging leaders who still await the care of spiritual parents. Ellie and I have become mentors to many young men and women. We are compelled to be friends who will never use them for our personal gain. Our recent experience with a house/café church has especially exposed the critical need for young women to experience the genuine fathering of Godly men. So many of them have been abused by self-centered men and need a picture of Jesus "with skin on" to help them relate to a heavenly Father. I walk with gratitude in the shadow of Grampa Davey and Uncle Eric and others who have shown a genuine interest in me with no secret agenda of their own.

What would the church look like if every spiritual leader was devoted to reaching out to emerging leaders with an authentic desire for their success? What wonderfully creative expressions of church would emerge under the leadership of a "mothered and fathered" generation? What would have become of Christianity if Jesus had not made that kind of commitment to the young, emerging leaders around Him?

THREE:

There's a Train 'a Coming!

There is no fear in love;
but perfect love casts out fear,
because fear involves punishment.
1 John 4:18 NASB

Is the gospel primarily an invitation
to escape the flames of hell
and access the rewards of heaven?
DH

I got *saved* almost every summer at camp; it was pretty much expected of us rowdy, young boys. Most of us would hold out until the very last altar call was given while the young girls pleaded with us to get right with God or get left behind when the imminent "rapture" took place. I still remember some of the emotionally intense moments at the "with this I close" finale of an impassioned sermon. One in particular stands out in my mind. The evangelist was concluding a fiery message that had made me quite uncomfortable about sneaking a kiss from my little girlfriend the night before. As was often the case, he began a countdown to narrow the moments that we had left to come to the altar. With each descending number he would stop and tell another story about someone who had not "come forward" in his past meetings, and the tragic events that immediately closed in upon them. He was finally at "one" and he had saved the best story until the end. Wiping the perspiration from his brow with a white handkerchief, he told us this story.

In one of his meetings as he gave one last chance to respond to "God", he said that he knew that a certain young lady needed to come forward. He announced that this was her last chance. About then, a young lady got up from her pew and headed out the back door. To my utter shock, he said that she was immediately struck by a passing freight train, was killed, and went straight to Hell. There was an uneasy silence that gripped the room. My mind wandered back to the time that the church was built; I just couldn't get over the fact that they built the church right at the edge of the railroad tracks, or that they had allowed the railroad to lay their tracks so close to the church. Why would they do that? This just didn't make sense to me. Where was this church anyways? Maybe they should consider a side entrance away from the train tracks. I guess that I had somehow missed his point; worse yet he had begun the closing prayer and I hadn't "gone forward." As I left the church that night I opened the door carefully and looked both ways for trains or buses or trucks or cars or fire and brimstone. I often had the *"Hell"* scared out of me at camp meetings!

Is the gospel primarily an invitation to escape the flames of hell and access the rewards of heaven? The political history of the world is filled with examples of leaders who understood two methods of controlling people. *Reward and punishment* are powerful ways to get people to do your bidding. If you do what I want you to do I will give you food or shelter or land or certain freedoms or whatever is at my disposal to use. If you do not do what I want, you will be punished with physical, emotional, mental or spiritual pain. These two methods have been very effective in the hands of rulers for centuries.

Fear is a tool of control. If I live my life under a cloud of fearfulness, I am neutralized in my ability to fulfill destiny. The true essence of the gospel, if it is "good news" must transcend the choice between rewards and punishment. It must be more than a set of rules to be kept, a system of rights and wrongs to be followed. It must be something closer to "perfect love", a relationship to share, a friendship to enjoy!

The gospel is so much more than a message that is proclaimed to try to get people to give assent to a list of beliefs. It is really a *love story* in which we are participants. It tells of a loving Father who wants to share His heart of fellowship with a new breed of creatures which He has created and placed in a beautiful home. It is about the creature's choice to rebel against everything that is good and perfect and whole. It is the story of a broken-hearted Father in pursuit of a lost creation, the ultimate overture being the *incarnation* of His son, coming in our creature-form to help us find our way back home. This story is about a Father's love, not his tyrannical anger because of our rebellion. This story is about a relationship of *love and trust*. I can love Father because He is full of goodness, I can trust Him because He is so wise. I can do nothing to deserve this immense gift. This gift is available to everyone. This is the gospel: the good news that allows me to step outside of any building without fearing the scream of a train whistle or the pungent smell of burning sulfur.

Inviting someone to join us as followers of Christ must be about far more than coercing them into making an initial decision to "accept" Him into their hearts, or to repeat a "sinner's prayer" that we have prepared beforehand. A couple of years ago I had preached in an inner-city church in Regina, Saskatchewan. During the prayer time after the service, I heard a man shout out with a very loud voice saying, "Jesus Christ, would you please get the f—- into my heart!" This was not your customary sinner's prayer, so it attracted a bit of attention, especially from me. The dear altar worker had invited the well-tattooed man to pray from his *own* heart, with his own words, to invite Jesus to come in. He proceeded to do exactly that! As I spent time with him later that evening and early before each service in the next few days, I learned that he had just been released from a Canadian Federal prison that week. He wanted to get his life sorted out, had opened the yellow pages in his hotel room looking for a church to attend, and had seen flaming words rise off the page telling him to go to that church.

Each time we met he had wonderful questions about scriptures he had read that day: "What the Hell does circumcision have to do with, Pastor Doug, and what does it mean to be filled with the Holy Spirit?" I must tell you that this whole event caused a number of issues to surface in me. I was offended by his language, especially in church. I judged his sincerity because of his vocabulary. I was certain that God was *at least* as offended as I was.

Then I heard God speak deeply within my own soul. He pointed out that I was so *religious* in my approach to seekers that I had made pre-conditions and formulas to assure that they would come to Christ through my methods. He assured me that this dear brother had come with a sincere heart, with an authentic sinner's prayer, and had entered the Kingdom of God, to His great delight. I was ashamed.

God is a loving, caring being. He longs to re-connect with women and men who have walked away from Him in rebellion. The depth of His love and breadth of His acceptance exceed anything that my little mind could imagine. He doesn't need my *salesmanship* to attract people to Himself. He really wants my life to speak with a sincere gratitude for what He has done for me. That is the good news!

FOUR:

Calling

*Walk in a manner worthy of the calling
with which you have been called.*
Ephesians 4:1 NASB

*Why do we worship a grey-toned conformity
in calling and ministry expression,
when His creative genius has given us
a full-color pallet of unique shades and hues?*
DH

How could I ever forget my third birthday! The little toy milk truck that I had unwrapped had tiny cases filled with miniature, removable milk bottles. As I drove the truck around on the table, I stopped occasionally to sell a bottle of milk for a penny to my dad or mom. Entrepreneurial blood flowed in my veins at a very early age. But soon my energy was gone and I needed to lie down again in my hospital bed.

Fifty five years ago, *spinal meningitis* was a life-threatening disease that required me to be in isolation. I remember the day that the nurse took me down a long hallway and gently assured me that I was going to be fine. As I was laid on the table, being held down by my nurse, I glanced over my shoulder just in time to see the largest, scariest needle of all time in the hand of my doctor. The indescribable fear and pain that followed as that enormous blade of steel penetrated my tiny back and spinal chord, imprinted itself upon my soul. I hate needles!

The dear folks of the local Pentecostal church had formed a prayer chain that placed someone at the church every hour of the day and night to pray for my healing. I had developed a very high temperature that lasted for many days. The doctors had informed my parents that my survival was questionable, and my condition if I survived would undoubtedly include either or mental incapacity, or both. (Over the years I have told friends that it is obvious that I suffered no *physical* disability from this). The church folks prayed, and one day I climbed out of my crib to look down upon hundreds of miniature cars in the parking lot below my window. I had been healed and I was going home!

It was now the summer of 1966. I stood at the altar at Braeside Camp, surrendering my life and future to God. My plans included enrolling in the engineering program at the University of Waterloo, Canada's finest engineering school, whose founder and first president just happened to be my father's cousin, Gerald G. Hagey. Swiss-German roots on my father's side had given me a linearly logical mind that would be a great asset. But, my plans got altared that summer. Within the depths of my soul I clearly heard a gentle, yet direct command to "Go to Bible School!" This had not crossed my mind before, had not been a part of any conscious desire, but I knew that this was God speaking.

As a young person you wonder what your parents' response will be to announcements about your own destiny. Dad responded with an *old world* German, Mennonite flair when he said, "Your Grampa would roll over in his grave with this news!" I tried to picture exactly how that would look, with old bones twisting and turning to get more comfortable in that narrow box. I wasn't exactly sure how to interpret that comment, but assumed that it must be a good thing to get a rise from the dead. Mom was a gentle, kind, British lady. Her response was one of great joy accompanied by an interesting confirmation that she had pondered for about fifteen years.

While I was in critical condition as a three year old, a wonderful older lady in the church had prophesied to my parents that I would not die, and that God had a calling on my life for ministry. Not wanting to push me in that direction, my parents had withheld that story until this moment in my life. God had spoken to me personally, had spoken about me through one of his servants many years before, and had now confirmed direction by bringing the two together. I was amazed and humbled.

So now it was time to begin preparing myself for college. I had fantasized for years about riding into the sunset on a motorcycle. Every time a biker passed by I was whisked away in my mind with pictures of my manly form commanding the pilot seat of a roguish cycle. At one point in time I had responded to an advertisement for a cheap motorcycle. When I arrived at the house, I could see three, very large, leather-clad men working on an enormous machine. When I enquired about the bike for sale, they stepped aside to reveal the biggest, *"baddest"* Harley Davidson I had ever seen. I was shocked at its size; they were shocked that I was there. In gentle, but direct language, they encouraged me to find something a bit smaller. Apparently my 140 pound frame would not have been a match for this steel dragon. I appreciated their genuine concern and settled for a much smaller version.

After finishing my senior year in high school, it was time to head for Peterborough and Eastern Pentecostal Bible College. I needed to sell my little Bridgestone 50cc step-through motorbike. The license had expired, but I had taken it to Ellie's house to get it ready for sale. Late that night I decided to head home, riding my bike on smaller side streets so as not to be intercepted by the police. Part way home, my heart leapt into my throat as a bright light shone into my face as a police car pulled up beside me. No license plate, no insurance, I was going to jail! The officer told me to push the bike the rest of the way downtown to the police station, where he would be waiting for me. That was one of the longest journeys of my life. How could I have been so foolish? How much would the fines be? How could I tell him that I was selling the bike to go to "Bible" school? Would my friends and parents visit me in jail?

The officer recited a rather long list of offences, each punishable with substantial fines. I pleaded my case with sincerity and honesty. I was wrong in what I had done. I was heading to Bible school and desperately needed the money from the sale of my bike to pay for tuition. I was from a *nice* family that went to church regularly. I liked policemen. I had never done anything to break the law before now (Well, there was that one incident of shooting arrows straight up into the sky). I had a girlfriend. I had been the mayor-for-a-day of our town and had been in charge of the police department for a few hours. I dropped the puck for the opening game of the Paris Junior 'C' season. I would have given him a raise if I had been the *real* mayor.

I am not sure what changed his mind, but he sent me home with a warning to never ride unlicensed again, and best wishes for my future as a minister. I have never again experienced that level of sheer awkwardness.

Calling is an important doorway into fulfilling destiny, but character is in many ways more important than any other aspect of ministry. I had grown up in a church that placed great emphasis upon the "Gifts of the Spirit". Tongues, interpretation, and prophecy held high value in our religious system. These gifts were given to us to do the works of Christ.

I have come to realize that the "Fruit of the Spirit" that describe the character of Jesus, are essential in our lives if we want to be like Jesus. How many times have gifted, spiritual leaders fallen from grace because they lacked character? I was leaving town to train for the ministry to which I felt called, but I would never forget those moments standing before justice, with my character exposed to the light.

My daughter Tonya was reading a book this past week that she shared with me for a few hours, long enough to be captivated by its message. Parker J. Palmer has written this wonderful little book titled: **Let Your Voice Speak – Listening For The Voice Of Vocation** (2000, Jossey-Bass, A Wiley Co., San Francisco, CA 94103). He writes:

> *Vocation does not mean a goal that I pursue. It means a calling that I hear. Before I can tell my life what I want to do with it, I must listen to my life telling me who I am. (4)*
>
> *(An approach other than this is) a distortion of my true self – as must be the case when one lives from the outside in, not the inside out. (3)*
>
> *…running beneath the surface of the experience I call my life, there is a deeper and truer life waiting to be acknowledged. (5)*
>
> *What a long time it can take to become the person one has always been. How often in the process we mask ourselves in faces that are not our own. (9)*
>
> *Vocation does not come from a voice "out there" calling me to become something I am not. It comes from a voice "in here" calling me to be the person I was born to be, to fulfill the original selfhood given me at birth by God. (10)*

The punishment imposed on us for claiming true self can never be worse than the punishment we impose on ourselves by failing to make that claim. (34)

When I stand before God, I won't be asked "Why were you not Billy Graham?", but rather, "Why were you not Doug Hagey?" The beauty of diversity is God's idea from creation itself. Why do we worship a grey-toned conformity in calling and ministry expression, when His creative genius has given us a full-color pallet of unique shades and hues?

FIVE:

Information or Formation?

My children,
with whom I am again in labor
until Christ is formed in you.
Galatians 4:19-20 NASB

It is my personal belief that there are
two essential paths that must be visited in
education.
One is of course the sharing of information,
the other is the forming of character.
DH

B ible College...here I come! It was quite a thrill to be driving off to Peterborough, Ontario and Eastern Pentecostal Bible College. I had graduated from Grade thirteen (yes... it takes longer to get smart in Ontario) with honors, and looked forward to the challenge of higher education. There was a level of anxiety as well, because I had struggled with reading and found it difficult to concentrate on any one thing for very long. I knew that there would be volumes to read and many papers to write.

My first semester was not the ordeal that I had envisioned. I found the course work to be quite easy, the assignments doable and the exams undemanding. My second semester was more devoted to basketball, hockey and socializing than to studies. By my second year I lacked the energy and initiative that was needed to keep up with my classes and workload. Then, I had Virgil Gingrich as a teacher. He was different, he was speaking into my life, not just my head. He forced me to reflect on my faith, not simply to collect information about it. I was confronted with the relationship between truth and spirit, between what I knew and what affect that knowledge had on my life. As a result of his influence I regained my focus and passion for being there.

Why have some settled for the notion that Bible College education is primarily the pulling together of a collection of facts, knowledge and truth from which we can draw conclusions? This idea has led to well-constructed sermons, but often to poorly constructed lives. It is my personal belief that there are two essential paths that must be visited in education. One is of course the sharing of information, the other is the forming of character. Both are important! Information without formation can lead to a prideful attitude of superiority, an inability to apply truth to lifestyle, and a disconnection from the real-life issues of people around us. Formation without information can lead to error and ignorance, although a woman or man of character recognizing their lack of knowledge, would likely pursue truth from a heart of faithfulness and devotion to Christ.

When I attended Central Bible College in Springfield, Missouri, I was privileged to attend a class with Opel Reddin. (I describe her contribution more fully in Part Three). She understood the important dual focus of education. I came away from her classes with a deep sense of being formed and shaped for ministry, not simply filled with more knowledge.

In 1995, Rick Warren wrote *The Purpose Driven Church* (Zondervan, Grand Rapids, Michigan 49530). In a small paragraph (which he expanded in a later book) he described this idea of being "formed" for ministry. He used the acrostic "S-H-A-P-E" to express his thoughts. I was captivated by this expansion of the traditional "spiritual gifts" assessments that I had used in the past. He begins where I had spent most of my time, and goes far beyond that.

"S" is *spiritual gifts*. There are a great many books and teachings on this subject, the basic thought being that Christ has given a variety of gifts to the church to help us function with different expressions, to create a unique unity flowing from our diversity. Some writers and teachers place much emphasis on the "Big 5" gifts of Ephesians 4:11 (apostles, prophets, evangelists, pastors, teachers). Others, like C. Peter Wagner (2002, ***Discover Your Spiritual Gifts***, Regal Books, Ventura, California) have noted over twenty-five gifts mentioned in scripture. The bottom line is that we are not all the same in the church, we bring our own portion to the whole, and what we bring helps the whole church to grow.

"H" is *heart or passion*. There could be a group of people in a room who all have the gift of teaching, for example. They could all express that gift in different contexts, with different age groups, with creative differences of expression. I mentioned my Uncle Eric in a previous chapter. He was a gifted teacher. His passion was to teach young boys in Sunday school using hands-on, active learning techniques. Opel Reddin, also a gifted teacher, was passionate about teaching emerging leaders in Bible College by asking searching questions and drawing out the deep, inner thoughts of our souls. Both were teachers, but with different expressions of their gift because of their heart's passion.

"A" is *abilities*. I can play chopsticks on the piano on a good day, but I have heard the incredible sounds coming from a grand piano the keys of which are being caressed by the fingers of a gifted concert pianist. We all have abilities in different areas of life, with differing degrees of talent. We can accelerate in those abilities by training and hard work, but there will still be the good, the better and the best.

"P" is *personality*. This has been a life-long study for many, and volumes of books and tests have been written on the subject. The variety of approaches parallels the variety of personalities: introverts – extroverts, feelers – thinkers, type A – type B, coleric – sanguine, red – green, intuitive – judging, artisans – rationals. Someone has even compared personality types to animals: Lions are the assertive leaders, Otters are the social, relationship types, Golden Retrievers are the sensitive, caring team players, and Beavers are the organized, methodical analysts. Isn't variety wonderful? The main point is that we express who we are in a great assortment of ways when it comes to our personalities.

"E" is *experience*. This part of who we are is affected by our age, environment, ethnic background, gender, education, parenting, and so on. We each bring our special story, our journey, into how we present ourselves to others in work and ministry. There are some things that many of us share in common, but many of our experiences, and how they have affected us, are unique to us alone.

Warren helped me to appreciate the multi-faceted formation that takes place in all of our lives over time. I am not simply the recipient of a spiritual gift that must be expressed in a prescribed manner in the church. I minister out of the process of my own unique development as a person. This is refreshing!

While attending Fuller Seminary, I was introduced to a life-changing book, ***The Making of a Leader*** by Dr. J. Robert Clinton (1988, Navpress, Colorado Springs, CO 80935). After studying the lives of hundreds of historical, biblical and contemporary leaders, Clinton identifies six primary stages of leadership development and key checkpoints to help you find out where you are in the process. This is a little bit like entering a large shopping mall and viewing the directory that is placed near the entry point. The first thing you look for is the arrow that says, "You are here." The idea that captivated my attention in his book was that we are all walking a unique, God-directed timeline, with our own set of circumstances and people and opportunities to help in the process of molding us into leaders. We experience both joy and pain in this process, each contributing to who we are becoming. The thought of a caring Father personally guiding a child through the maze of life's perplexities, with the unselfish goal of bringing that child to his or her fullest potential is somewhat overwhelming. I was finally able to place the painful moments in my ministry life into the much broader context of leadership development. I was able to revisit the "boundary events" that moved me from one stage into the next, with an understanding that God was walking with me in the entire timeline. I am being formed by a God who invests Himself in me and my future; I am not alone! Clinton writes:

> *Effective spiritual ministry flows out of being, and God is concerned with our being. He is forming it. The patterns and processes He uses to shape us are worthwhile subjects for leadership study. (13)*
>
> *Leadership is a dynamic process in which a man or woman with God-given capacity influences a specific group of God's people toward His purposes for the group. To be considered a leader, one does not require a professional position nor need to be a 'full-time' Christian worker. (14)*
>
> *When you look on leadership development in terms of life's processes, you quickly realize who the academic dean really is. It is God. Each of us has*

leadership courses that are tailored for us by the Academic Dean. (15-16)

Leadership is a lifetime of God's lessons. It is not a set of do-it-yourself correspondence courses that can be worked through in a few months or years. Yours will be unique. God will take you through several 'leadership stages' on your way to a lifetime of service. (27, 40)

In her 1992 book **A Return to Love** (Harper Collins Publishers, New York, NY) Marianne Williamson writes these haunting thoughts:

Our deepest fear is not that we are inadequate,
Our deepest fear is that we are powerful beyond measure,
It is our light, not our darkness that most frightens us.
We ask ourselves, "Who am I to be brilliant, gorgeous, talented and fabulous?"
Actually, who are you not to be?
You are a Child of God.
Your playing small does not serve the world.
There is nothing enlightened about shrinking so other people won't feel insecure about you.
We were born to manifest the glory of God that is within us.
It's not just in some of us; it's in everyone.
And as we let our light shine, we unconsciously give other people permission to do the same.
As we are liberated from our fear, our presence automatically liberates others.

SIX:

Jesus People

*You did not recognize
the time of your visitation.*
Luke 19:44 NASB

*Why would He choose to visit
flower children and hippies
when He has a church to work through?*
DH

In Paris, Ontario there sat the remains of the old Penman's Plant that provided jobs for many of the town's residents over the years. Great underwear came out of those doors. Changes from water power to electricity and manual labor to automation and growing competition from other producers had left parts of the mill abandoned. A number of revived young people thought this would be a wonderful setting for a Jesus People Café and drop-in center. Mismatched pieces of donated carpet and empty wire spools from the Hydro Company painted in bright colors made for an attractive environment, especially for hippies.

I was inspired to add my own creative contribution by painting a trilogy of watercolors that depicted the unfolding of The Creation. The frames were hand made from some old pieces of cedar and I hung them in the old mill with a sense of artistic accomplishment. These kids made us feel that we belonged with them. Ellie and I had just returned from a year at Central Bible College in Springfield, Missouri with a strong sense of direction to focus our ministry on young people.

We visited often with this growing group of young seekers of truth. It was refreshing to interact with them, to freely discuss our faith, our doubts, and our hope for a community of followers of Jesus who were more like the originals than what the church had become. The experience of being with young people who were so unabashedly real, transparent and hungry for an authentic faith brought such a pure joy to our hearts. Were we approaching God's idea of church for the first time in our lives?

During this time, we began to read articles in Look and **Time Magazine** that described other young people, especially in California, who were so dramatically changed by personal faith in Christ that even the secular media had noticed. We sifted through the encouraging articles with our hearts leaping within us. What could all of this mean? Was there some universal visitation from God happening around the world in which we had become participants?

The June, 1971 Time Magazine (Canadian Issue) featured a full front cover sketch of Jesus with the caption, "The Jesus Revolution." Amidst articles about Nixon's Vietnamization and withdrawal program, and Solzhenitsyn's newest book being released in the West, there was no less than twelve full pages of pictures and text under the title, "The New Rebel Cry: Jesus Is Coming!" It is fascinating to read a secular appraisal of what was happening in those days. I am including a series of excerpts so you can feel the significance of what was reported.

> *There is an uncommon morning freshness to this movement, a buoyant atmosphere of hope and love along with the usual rebel zeal. Some converts seem to enjoy translating their new faith into everyday life, like those who answer the phone with "Jesus loves you" instead of "hello." But their love seems more sincere than a slogan, deeper than the fast-fading sentiments of the flower children; what startles the outsider is the extraordinary sense of joy that they are able to communicate.*
>
> *If any one mark clearly identifies them it is their total belief in an awesome, supernatural Jesus Christ, not just a marvelous man who lived 2000 years ago but a living God who is both Savior and Judge, the ruler of their destinies. Their lives revolve around the necessity for an intense personal relationship with that Jesus, and the belief that such a relationship should condition every human life. They act as if divine intervention guides their every movement and can be counted on to solve every problem.*
>
> *"If it is a fad", says Evangelist Billy Graham, "I welcome it."*
>
> *There are signs that the movement is something quite a bit larger than a theological Hula-Hoop, something more lasting than a religious Woodstock. It cuts across nearly all the social dividing lines, from crew cut to long hair, right to left, rich to poor.*
>
> *Clergymen like Houston's John Bisagno, even when [he is] uncertain of the full meaning and the life span of the Jesus revolution, says, "All I know is that kids are turning on to Jesus. My concern is that*

the staid, traditional churches will reject these kids and miss the most genuine revival of our lifetime."
In a world filled with real and fancied demons for the young, the form their faith takes may be less important than the fact that they have it. Ronald Knox, who set out in Enthusiasm to expose the heresies of religious enthusiasts, concluded by praising their spirit. "How nearly we thought we could do without St. Francis, without St. Ignatius," he ended his work, "Men will not live without vision, that moral we would do well to carry away with us from contemplating, in so many strange forms, the record of the visionaries."
Enthusiasm may not be the only virtue, but God knows, apathy is none at all." (Time Canada, June 21, 1971 Pages 36-47)

Look Magazine contributed their version of this story in their February 9, 1971 edition. A seven page article began with a picture of young people with raised hands joined together in worship. The bold caption read, "The Jesus Movement Is Upon Us!" Here are a few quotes from that edition.

A crusade – a massive, fundamentalist, Christ-as-personal-Savior revival – has caught hold in California, and it shows every sign of sweeping East and becoming a national preoccupation. It's an old-time, Bible-toting, witness-giving kind of revival, and the new evangelists are the young. They give their Christian message with cheerful dedication: Turn on to Jesus. He's coming Soon.
The Jesus movement seems to be springing up simultaneously in a miscellany of places, and often in the last places you would think to look. In Orange

County, an entire motorcycle gang converted. In Anaheim, a huge entertainment complex called Melodyland has been taken over by a nondenominational, solidly middle-class religious group. Dozens of go-go clubs throughout the state have been turned into religious coffee-houses, where kids go to sing and pray.

This is a movement that started subtly – almost secretly, as if religion's widespread unfashionableness made faith a bit felonious.

It's a revival, there's no getting around it. Jesus is rising in California. He's the latest movement, the latest thing to groove on. Ministers who have been trying to lure young people into their churches for years say it's like an express train rushing by. Some of them jump on and some just watch. (Look, February 9, 1971, Pages 15-21)

This movement found a variety of expressions. While we were at Central Bible College, we read the report of a wonderful transformation taking place at Asbury College in Wilmore, Kentucky. The book, **One Divine Moment**, (1970, Robert E. Coleman, Fleming H. Revell Co., Grand Rapids, MI 49516) chronicled God's visitation at a chapel service that involved spontaneous, public confessions by students and faculty that resulted in extended prayer and worship day and night for weeks. This affected dozens of other campuses around the country as student leaders came to witness this revival and carried its fervor back with them to their own campuses.

There was a deep stirring in our hearts as we read about God's reviving work among the youth in California. As difficult as it was to uproot from family and the familiar, we knew that we wanted to be in the middle of whatever He was doing in our day. We were invited to fill a position as youth and music director at a church in Fresno, California in the Fall of 1972. We were about to be in the middle of it all, complete with our own orange and grapefruit trees.

That was a remarkable time to be alive! Young people were coming to faith with little effort or planned evangelism involved. The little, struggling youth group grew from a dozen to ten dozen in a few weeks. We painted a large room in a beautiful purple, ping-pong tables in a darker purple with bright yellow balls. Stitched pieces of random carpet (mostly that long stringy, shag-style) and bean-bag pillows formed a more intimate gathering place in a side room. My office was a deep, metallic blue auto paint. The full-wall logo at the front of the chapel was a huge globe with a hand with index finger pointed upward superimposed on a dove in flight. Above and below the logo was the caption, "One Way." We were having the time of our lives. Church was fun!

During this same time, a number of new churches such as Calvary Chapel were bursting into existence, as they embraced this remarkable visitation. A handful of existing churches like Melodyland welcomed these new Christians into their ranks. Sadly though, many mainline churches and denominations rejected the people of this movement mostly on the basis of the external differences of dress and hair length. Personal preference became theological separation. Aberrant groups sprang up as a protest against the rigidity of the established church. Without the loving nurture of spiritual fathers and mothers, many of the new followers fell back into old lifestyles of sexual and drug addictions, only this time in groups whose leaders preached a 'free love' theology from scripture. This is the painful epitaph to this otherwise amazing story.

We had experienced a touch of the Divine. God's visitation had stimulated joyful love of the brethren, spontaneity of worship and relationship, contagious sharing of personal faith, passionate hunger to know God, and a genuine devotion to build His church.

What surprised me was the level of rejection from many existing churches. What was so important to protect, that they would miss a real movement of grace? Were these wide-eyed, spiritually-activated youth a threat to the churches?

I have come to the conclusion over the years that the next move of God is always criticized and rejected by the people of the last move of God. Surely if God was going to do something new He would do it through those who have already experienced His moving in the past. Why would He choose to visit a small cluster of people meeting in an old airplane hanger in the remote town of North Battleford, Saskatchewan in 1948, when there were plenty of real churches around? Why would He choose to visit flower children and hippies in 1968 when He had churches with buildings to work through? Why would He choose to pour out His Spirit upon mainline denominations in the seventies and eighties when the Pentecostals have had that experience for years? Why would He visit a small church in Toronto, Canada in 1994, when there were mega-churches all over the United States?

The painful reality seems to be that we welcome God to revive us as long as it is within our established structures, with familiar experiences that do not disrupt our plans and schedules. When an apparent visitation does not fit our criterion, we reject it, criticize it or simply ignore it. The now broken people who once sought church *family* during times of God's visitation, but were rejected, are the witnesses to our parochialism.

SEVEN:

Tent Tea

*Do not neglect
to show hospitality
to strangers.*
Hebrews 13:2 NASB

*If church is not the friendliest place on earth
are we kidding ourselves
about the value and meaning of our faith?*
DH

We had already experienced the jolt of having the neighbor's tent blown through the air and settle atop our own. Then there was the abundance of rainfall in the same farmer's field in Holland that left our suitcases floating inside our tent like small ships in the night. There was nothing that felt either secure or permanent for our little family of four. We had all acquired *klompens* (brightly colored, carved, wooden clogs) to keep our feet dry while sloshing through the mud on our way to the YWAM food and meeting tent. The locals seemed quite impressed as they watched our daughter running at full speed in her wooden shoes.

Ellie and I had both grown up in families that valued hospitality. Every day my mother had taken a hot meal to a ninety year old neighbor lady. Mrs. Hollingsworth had nothing to give in return, her life was sustained by the quiet, gentle care of a lady who sought no reward for her gifts. Ellie's family often provided meals and housing for missionaries on furlough and international Bible school students needing a home during special holidays. Her mother's reputation apparently was broadly known so that even the occasional *false missionary* showed up to receive their kind and generous hospitality. There was a time when Ellie's dad was searching his closet for one of his suits, and finally asked if anyone knew where it was. The answer came quickly, that it was walking down the tracks in the possession of a happy, railroad Hobo. This devotion to caring for others had influenced our values and had become a part of our own lifestyle.

How does one show hospitality while living in a nine foot square tent, in a muddy field in Holland, or in a parking lot in Belgium, or in a campsite in southern France? We discovered that we could heat a small pot of tea over our little propane heater. We started to invite young couples from the neighboring tents to join us "at our place" for tent tea. There was nothing elaborate or fancy about those times, but they were wonderful times of connecting and developing friendships while seated cross-legged on the vinyl floor of a tent, sipping tea.

This whole idea of sharing meals in each other's homes is rooted in the early church. There is something very special that happens when we sit together around a meal in each other's home environment. Restaurant food is fine, but even lesser cuisine in a home carries with it some unique benefits. When we invite someone into our home, they come under our care and protection. They get to see our household up close. We've noticed that we can always count on our children to divulge any family secrets or bad habits, or to publicly correct us on any story that isn't told with absolute faithfulness to the facts during the visit. Our guests experience an inside look into the realm that we consider our haven from the outside world. Many people have expressed a desire to have an open home, but have never followed through because of feeling embarrassed about what they have to offer.

I will admit that there are degrees of hospitality. I remember a time when we were traveling in ministry, visiting many churches in a short period of time. In one church, we arrived just in time for the meeting with no time to eat a meal. After an intense meeting with many people wanting prayer, we were connected with our host family. When we arrived at their home, we had to ask where we would be staying, and eventually for a drink, which turned out to be water. The family went about their routine as if we weren't even there. We were never asked if we were hungry, or if there was anything we needed. Being tired from travel and ministry, we decided to head for bed. When we pulled back the sheets, it was very obvious that the sheets had been well used by others before us, and that they had not recently seen the inside of a washing machine. We learned the next day that our original hosts had a last minute change of plans, and that we were placed with a somewhat hesitant family who had never done anything like this before. Why were we chosen to be the experimental guinea pigs? Another lesson I would guess.

The key to hospitality was summarized a number of years ago in a book, ***Open Heart, Open Home*** (Karen Mains, 1976, Intervarsity Press, Downers Grove, IL 60515). The subtitle was, "The Hospitable Way to Make Others Feel Welcome and Wanted." The book's premise is that it is the openness of our hearts that makes our home an open place to others. Back in the "dirty sheets" and "water-for-supper" home, we felt neither welcome nor wanted. It reminded me of the words of Jesus when being criticized for allowing an extravagant gift of perfume to be poured on his feet and then dried with a woman's hair. He looked into the hearts of those who pointed accusing fingers and simply said:

> *Do you see this woman? I entered your house; you gave Me no water for My feet, but she has wet My feet with her tears, and wiped them with her hair. You gave Me no kiss, but she, since the time I came in, has not ceased to kiss My feet. You did not anoint My head with oil, but she anointed My feet with perfume. For this reason I say to you, her sins, which are many, have been forgiven, for she loved much; but he who is forgiven little, loves little.*
> Luke 7:44-48 NASB

Jesus makes a direct link between the issues of our heart, which include our view of forgiveness, and our ability to love others. How did God approach us with forgiveness? It was on the basis of another extravagant gift that was given freely to us, totally contrasting anything we deserved. To the extent that we value that gift and maintain a gratefully responsive heart, we will love much. There are some simple, basic skills that can be learned to improve our hospitality, but having an open heart is the beginning.

Some of the words used to describe hospitality include: reception, greeting, welcome, warmth, kindness, generosity, helpfulness and thoughtfulness. This list sounds strangely similar to the Fruit of the Spirit listed in Galatians 5: 22-23. Establishing the foundation of a loving heart is a prerequisite to building any ministry. Hospitality flowing from a loving heart responds to our humanity, our need to feel welcome and wanted.

We have had the opportunity to visit many dozens of churches in the United States and Canada and in several other countries. Some were multi-cultural, some mono-cultural, some were large, some very small, some were part of a denomination, some independent. The one obvious distinction between them was their ability to entertain strangers. Some of the most unfriendly churches had websites and handouts that boasted that they were the friendliest place in town, but when we visited, we were not welcomed by anyone, and left the building unnoticed and feeling less-than-human. It is important to point out that there was laughter and fellowship and friendship happening all around us, but we were ignored. The advertising for these churches should say that after you become a member and join some activity group within the church, you will have a small circle of friends that will make you feel welcome and wanted. Maybe they won't do that.

For a long time I was critical of the idea of "professional greeters"; you know those people at the door with the big brass name plate on their chest that identifies them as "Greeter". Then, I got to know some of those folks and discovered that many of them live and breathe for that opportunity to come up each week. They are using their gifts and their open heart to genuinely create an atmosphere that says from the outset that you are welcome there. It is their authenticity that reaches into our humanity.

It is the leaders of churches who must set patterns and model hospitality. In one church that we pioneered, we would invite every new family (after they had visited for a couple of weeks) to our home for dinner. This was a wonderful opportunity to hear their story, and for them to get behind the scene of ministry and into our daily lives. It was never difficult to encourage our church family to open their homes, having modeled that value from the beginning ourselves.

I remember visiting a church for the first time and the congregation was instructed by the pastor to form small prayer circles to share personal needs and then pray for one another. We had been in YWAM recently, and had been trained in the value and need for openness and brokenness in the church. Ellie and I turned to join hands with a middle-aged couple who didn't seem too enthused about this opportunity to "fellowship" in the middle of Sunday morning worship. So, we broke the ice with honest confessions of our shortcomings, with needs in our finances, and anything else that came to mind that needed prayer. Having finished exposing ourselves, we asked how we could pray for them. To our astonishment they replied that they had an "unspoken" request. It felt like one of those times when a group of friends decides to do something or shout something strange in a public place. On the count of three they all remain silent or seated while you shout out some foolish words or jump on your chair, totally alone and feeling rather foolish. We didn't know that there was this card in the deck called "unspoken request" that could be used whenever you didn't want to be open with other Christians. Ellie and I led in prayer in our little circle, everyone else was silent. The truth was that the pastor did not model hospitality himself, but tried to squeeze a hospitable moment into the Sunday morning event.

The whole idea of fellowship (a word once defined to me by a kind, retired pastor as "two fellows in a ship") is really a state of mind and heart, much more a lifestyle than an event. We have attended church fellowship dinners in many places. Some were nothing more than a group of hungry people eating too much home-cooked lasagna, with no conversation about life or faith or anything. Then, there were those memorable connections with strangers who opened their lives to us as if we were long-time friends catching up on each other's journey. I would be happy to eat bread and drink water with people whose personal faith is expressed in their entire lifestyle. Lasagna would be great too!

In Search of the Church

If church is not the friendliest place on earth are we kidding ourselves about the value and meaning of our faith? I had been told for years to never enter one of those "beer parlors" or hang around with the kind of people who frequent them. Last year a group of friends in Vancouver invited Ellie and me to join them for "fellowship" at an Irish pub downtown. We consented to join them in this "worldly" place. The fellowship was sweet, the food was great and the Irish band was amazing. To my utter shock and surprise I looked around a fully packed room to see people laughing and talking and hugging and greeting strangers and enjoying being themselves. This was not the picture embedded in my childhood mind of desperate drunkards, drooling in their beer, preparing to go home to abuse their family. Now I know that alcoholism is the cause of much pain and suffering and I would never minimize its sad affect on families, but this was something different. This was people hanging out together, enjoying life, sharing stories, being human. I was embarrassed as I recalled the many times that church folks met for "fellowship" that didn't come close to the joy and energy that I felt in that pub. Were these the people that our parents and pastors had warned us about? Why can't we be real with one another? If given the choice, would these "pub-people" go to a church fellowship time or stay in the pub?

Jim Henderson, Founder of Off the Map, has just co-authored a book: ***Jim and Casper Go to Church*** (2007, Barna Books, an imprint of Tyndale House Publishers, Inc., Carol Stream, IL 60188). Matt Casper, an atheist, and Jim, a long-time Christian leader, visited numerous churches together and then discussed what they saw, heard and felt. I highly recommend that you read this insightful book. Here are a couple of excerpts. Jim writes:

> *Casper saw and experienced - over and over and over again – what Christians do when they do church. He*

saw it done with big budgets and no budgets, in large stadiums and in small buildings. The same format repeated itself regardless of the setting. The greetsing-preach-collect-present form played out in front of us with unrelenting predictability. And when it was all done, he would turn to me and ask, "Jim, is this what Jesus told you guys to do?"

Casper writes:

The question that just came up for me again and again – having read more than a few pages of the Bible is this: What does the way Christianity is practiced today have to do with the handful of words and deeds uttered by a man who walked the earth two thousand years ago?

Indeed, Casper, what is the fellowship of the saints? How should we be devoted to one another in love? What does it mean to be poor in spirit, gentle, hungering and thirsting for righteousness, merciful, pure in heart and peacemakers? How can we be the salt of the earth and the light of the world? How can I love my enemy as well as my neighbor? How can I lay up treasures in heaven? How can I feel the compassion of Jesus for the distressed and downcast multitudes?

EIGHT:

Saturday Night Live and Beyond

*Being diligent
To preserve the unity
of the Spirit
in the bond of peace.*
Ephesians 4:3 NASB

*Trying to find your place
in an environment that is hostile
to new ways of thinking
can be overwhelming at times.*
DH

To say that we were naïve idealists in 1977 might be an understatement. In many ways we were inexperienced, immature and unsophisticated in our approach to ministry. Our romanticized view of what the church could be was uncomplicated and primitive.

We had experienced the joyful freedom of worship and community in Youth With A Mission in Lausanne, Switzerland and elsewhere. It was with this backdrop that we began to meet with a few friends on Saturday night at the local Methodist Church social hall in the small town of Dinuba, California. The format was simple: fellowship, worship and teaching. It grew to seventy-five adults very quickly. They had come from several denominational backgrounds and surrounding communities. These were joyful times, times of growing friendships, times of intimate worship, times of growth in personal faith, times of aligning lifestyle with Biblical truth. Then, the inevitable happened – actually, two *inevitables*!

Pastors began to hear about these "secret" meetings. We were "stealing sheep" from the household of faith. Why were we in competition with them? Did we not understand that they had certain "ownership rites" to these people?

Then some of the folks who were attending these fellowship times came to us to ask if this could become their church. They were experiencing something fresh and new and wanted it to be more than just a Saturday Night fellowship. They wanted us to be their *official* pastor.

My heart sank on both accounts. I loved my fellow pastors and had no desire or intention to offend them. We had chosen Saturday to not be in competition. We had done everything we knew how to do to make it just a fellowship group meeting in a relatively neutral location. We were so focused on wanting to experience authentic Christian community that we overlooked the rules that govern a divided church.

Secondly, we had come through a very difficult ministry appointment that had left us wary of pastoring, and fearful of the controlling attitudes of the few in charge who were opposed to change. When we left that position we said that we would never again pastor in a traditional church setting. The pain that we still carried became the stumbling-block to our forward movement. In the midst of these two responses, we decided to close it down, and walk away from what had become the closest expression of true community that we had witnessed.

The pain of previous experience so often blinds us from seeing the hope that lies right in front of us. We had bumped into this reality: many church-goers are unfulfilled, unhappy, unchallenged, underdeveloped, and frustrated because they do not know why they feel that way. Our little Saturday night experiment had exposed a real need for something fresh and new and real. There were many followers of Christ who desperately wanted to be more involved in doing His works and being more like Him. Sadly, our own history of striving for those very things had left us beaten up by a church that wanted all things to stay the same as they had always been. We had come so close! There had been a momentary flicker of the purest light exposing us to what could be.

Trying to find your place in an environment that is hostile to new ways of thinking can be overwhelming at times. We left the Dinuba area and began another phase of our pilgrimage, this time in east Texas.

The Agape Force was in many ways a resurrection of the earliest values of William and Catherine Booth, the founders of the Salvation Army. There was a militaristic precision to our lives, our housing and our schedules. A leader even visited our little rental home to check that all of our hangers were facing the same direction in our closet and that the house was spotless. At one point in our "training" we were dropped off in teams of four in one of the roughest and most dangerous areas of Dallas. Our "assignment" was to return after at least one conversion was recorded, and with more money than when we started. We were not permitted to tell anyone that we had need of food or housing or anything else.

The leader (by virtue of being a second year trainee) of our group was immediately stunned by the fact that we had been dropped into a neighborhood in which he had arrested many drug "salesmen" during his years on the Dallas NARC squad. His continuous "over-the-shoulder" surveillance brought a certain degree of concern to the rest of us.

That first night as we nestled close to each other in the local park, we were warned by several youth hanging out there that almost every night someone was stabbed, shot or otherwise made to feel abused in that park. Between "chigger" attacks (pesky little bugs that burrow into your skin) and noises that caused our minds to revisit horror movies we had seen as kids, we made it through our first restless night.

We connected the next day with a neighborhood church that gave us food, a place to shower, and floor space to sleep indoors. By Sunday, we spoke at that inner-city church, were guests on their radio show, prayed with folks to become followers of Jesus and walked away with a generous "love offering" from these wonderful people. I forgot to mention that we had to find our own way back to Lindale as well.

Para-church organizations, like the Agape Force and YWAM have existed for many years. Their roots sprang from the great divide between what the church has taught and what the church has actually done. Many young, non-conformist leaders have birthed movements to provide opportunity for "church kids" to be participants in the work of ministry. Their perception has been that the church has not fulfilled her role in things like evangelism, missions and mercy ministries, and that God has raised them up so that these essentials will not be overlooked.

It was in this para-church context that we clearly sensed God's direction to return to the place of "Saturday Night" fellowship and that He was going to raise up a new kind of church. We loaded up our little Opel station wagon, filled some gas cans to strap to the roof (this was a time of gas shortages) and headed west for California.

NINE:

The Wellspring Experiment

*Do not call to mind the former things,
Or ponder things of the past.
Behold I will do something new.*
Isaiah 43:18-19 NASB

*Sometimes starting from the very beginning
is the only way
that you can continue in ministry.*
DH

*Our failure to impact contemporary culture with
the gospel is not because
we have not been relevant enough,
but because we have not been
REAL enough.*
The Prodigal Project

It may seem too scientific and not very spiritual to call a church planting experience an experiment, but let me explain. I had tried to do church in all of the traditional ways, had tried to serve other men's visions, had tried to move into the future while tethered to unresolved historical issues between past leaders and their people. I felt a spiritual compulsion to start from scratch. There had to be a way of doing church that would be closer to the New Testament template, that would allow me the freedom to function within my spiritual gifts and passions, that would provide us with our own opportunity to make a history that we could understand and help direct.

In 1980 there was little instructional help available for church planters. We launched out into the unknown. We had a few thoughts about what we hoped church could be, but beyond that we were about to experiment with elements that we knew little about. Armed primarily with the idealism of risk-takers, and impacted by the beauty and simplicity of the picture we had of the early church in the Book of Acts, we decided that it was time, our time to bring something new to birth. I wish I could tell you that we knew what we were doing, or that we even knew how to begin this new thing. The reality is that we believed that God had brought us to the point of convergence between our frustration with the way things were and our deep desire for something more authentically faithful to the original. There have been a handful of times in our lives when the level of emotional and spiritual pain has become so high that it has led us to make major decisions about our future. This was one of those times!

I remember joking to Ellie that we should perhaps place an advertisement in the local newspaper stating that *Doug and Ellie are now receiving new church members. Would you like to be one of them?* Instead, we waited. If we learn to stay out of the way and keep our hearts and ears tuned to what God is saying, He will show us the next thing to do, if He is the originator of the direction.

The wonderful, young Nehf family who had recently become followers of Jesus contacted us and shared their need for a pastor. We had gotten to know them through other relationships, and they were without a church home at the time, and we heard God speaking through them. It was time to begin a new thing.

The living room in the old farmhouse we had rented had not been used in years. The floors were bare wood, the paint on the walls had reached retirement age years before, the windows were covered with old sheets, stained from the dampness of years of being in an unheated room. This would be our new church! We joyfully painted and carpeted and hung window coverings. A few scattered pieces of well-used furniture gave it that wonderful *lived-in* look. Sunday morning our two families came together to begin a different history.

I was introduced at the local Ministerial Association as the "founder" of a new, independent fellowship in town. It was quite apparent from the comments and the reception that some felt that another church was entirely unnecessary in a town with twenty-eight already in operation. It was strange to be *suspect* simply because I was not being placed there by some distant organization. I laid my cards face-up on the table that day: I was committed to the whole church in our community and would pray for God's blessing on each church and pastor, I was not in competition with any of them, I needed their fellowship, and I was an independent *thinker* without an independent *spirit*. I think some of that was disarming for them!

One of the discoveries that we made in the process of starting something new was that doing new things often means a return to doing old things with new insight and passion. Much of what we came to value was reclaimed from earlier times in church history.

From the outset of my introduction at the Ministerial Association, we sought to discover our place in the whole church. We saw ourselves as one part of the whole "body" that was the church in our community. When I shared with

In Search of the Church

my fellow pastors that I saw myself, and them, as elders of the same church, simply meeting in different places, it was at first viewed as a strange concept. Big surprise! So much of what we have done to the church over centuries of time has led to the exact opposite of "being diligent to preserve the unity of the Spirit in the bond of peace" (Ephesians 4:3 NASB). Amazingly, several of my brothers in ministry wanted to get together privately to fellowship and pray and confess faults and needs. When I was eventually asked to serve as their president, they encouraged me to lead them further into understanding the church in this more biblical way. To visit pastors in their office, many of them my senior in age and experience, and to feel a sense of brotherly love and care being mutually shared was a joyful connection for me. I was reminded often that God commands a blessing at the times and places that we pursue unity of the brethren (Psalm 133:1-3).

Over the next several years we would cooperate on a city-wide Luis Palau crusade that included a Sunday morning gathering of our churches in the local football stadium. A Youth With A Mission touring team made up of Island Breeze dancers, Kings' Kids and The Power Team spent a week in our community and the villages around it, sharing the good news. We purchased the "Jesus Video" for every household in our city and had a wonderful time of united prayer and distribution. We helped to sponsor a local shelter and food distribution program called "Open Gate", and a Youth for Christ leader to minister in our schools.

Learning how to promote and guard unity was an ongoing learning experience. A little later in our history, after my good friend and associate pastor Steve had become the senior pastor, Wellspring took a special Christmas Eve Sunday offering to give away to another church. The First Baptist Church was in a building program, attempting to pay as they went. They had a good portion of the building completed, but were stalled because of finances. Our church family gave the largest single offering in their history that Sunday morning. We all walked over to First Baptist, having informed the pastor that we had a "presentation" to make. As he closed the service, he invited us to come into their sanctuary, filling every isle and standing space around the perimeter. He later told us that he thought we were going to sing a special Christmas song for them. Steve simply presented Pastor Tom with our check as a gift to help them get on with their building. He was speechless, overwhelmed that a non-Baptist church would give $4600 to them. He had never heard of such a thing before in all his years as a Christian and a minister. People wept and laughed. We hugged and were hugged. A long time passed before we had all headed out the doors to be with our families for Christmas Eve.

This became the topic of conversation on the streets and in the shops downtown. The story appeared in the Foursquare Advance Magazine, the Baptist Standard and the local newspaper. The next Sunday, Pastor Tom encouraged his own people to respond to our giving with their own year-end gifts toward the project. They received thousands of dollars from their own people. Work began again and the building was soon completed. They invited our entire church to join them in celebrating its opening. They served us a wonderful meal in their new social hall. We felt like one family of followers of Jesus. This event should not be unique or unusual. We should all be committed to a costly unity with His church.

In our early days, I taught for many months on Gifts and Ministries in the church. I had never really witnessed the fulfillment of the Ephesians 4 idea of "that which every joint supplies." We constantly reminded people that when we gathered together, they had something to bring, not just receive. Sometimes someone would ask what the service would be like on Sunday. I would respond that I didn't know because I wasn't sure who would be there, and that would make a difference. We learned to love the unique blend of what different people had to bring. There was openness to public sharing of what God had been doing in our lives that past week. We came together with an expectation that God would speak to us in many different ways as we gathered.

I spent many Sundays sharing thoughts from the "One Another" commands of scripture (listed in the Introduction). There are many of them and they force us to apply truth to our lifestyle and relationships. A practical faith was emerging in our lives.

In the late 1970's when we were still trying to grasp the meaning of our Saturday Night fellowship, one of our brothers, Joe Peacock, shared a picture that God had impressed on his mind. He saw the church as an old Conestoga wagon wheel. The "hub" was the center into which we came for fellowship and training, the spokes were various avenues of reaching out into the world, the rim was the perimeter of our influence and the connection that we had together while outside of the hub. This idea became foundational to our understanding of the church. From this picture, God expanded our view of scripture into three primary thoughts. The Three Looks: Inward, Upward, Outward, became the basis from which we taught and approached ministry.

The Inward Look was illustrated by a person holding their heart in their hands before God. The teachings included personal faith, discipleship, purity of heart and so on. The Upward Look showed a person raising their heart to give it away to God. We taught about the character and greatness of God, the beauty and diversity of worship as an act and a lifestyle, and the value and meaning of prayer. The *Outward Look* was seen as a person giving their heart away to two groups of other people: one group representing followers of Jesus and the other representing those who were not yet followers. It became apparent that all of these overlap each other and often function simultaneously rather than in isolation from each other. As I live my life with authentic faith in Christ, I will naturally be connected with seekers and will be always aware of the presence and beauty of the Divine. The separation of these three into isolated segments of my life creates something less than God's intention for my faith walk. I was amazed as I began to view my life and church life through this grid. Scripture came alive as it informed us how to practice our faith in these three arenas.

As I studied and presented teachings on Gifts and Ministries, I was captivated by an idea from the story of Nehemiah's return to rebuild the broken walls around Jerusalem. Several enemies constantly taunted and ridiculed the workers. In Nehemiah 4 (NASB) we read:

> *Half of my servants carried on the work while half of them held the spears, the shields, the bows, and the breastplates.*
> *"The work is great and extensive, and we are separated on the wall far from one another. At whatever place you hear the sound of the trumpet, rally to us there. Our God will fight for us."*

I saw some with trowels and some with swords. Building and Battling were two key ideas from scripture that we needed to understand. We began to realize that some gifts and ministries (pastor, teacher, prophet, serving, administration) are given primarily for the "hub" to grow, while others (apostle, evangelist, missionary) are given as "go" gifts to extend the work of ministry out through the spokes to the perimeter. If we could grasp this truth, we would be mutually supportive of each other rather than in competition or being critical.

Within a few months of the birth of Wellspring, Willy and Diane Williams came to me to tell me that God was calling them to "go" and join YWAM. This was my test! They were involved in everything we were doing, were supportive of our leadership in every way, the "poster children" for loyalty, commitment and hard work. I thought of others whom I would prefer to "send", but there was an unmistakable calling on Willy and Diane's lives. They became our first full-time "missionaries" leaving the hub. Over the years they returned often on the "spoke" of committed relationship. Many others followed their example, and we became a church with influence around the globe that was totally disproportionate to the size of our little "hub" back in Dinuba, California.

One morning I received a phone call that began another learning experience for us as a young church. One of our leaders had just been arrested for embezzling a large sum of money from his employer. After my immediate reaction of shock, I asked God to show us how to walk through this impending process. The elders agreed that we needed to follow God's plan and in doing so to short circuit any scheme that gave Satan an opportunity to bring destruction. I met with the brother, and discerned that he was repentant and obviously broken by the foolishness of his actions.

I had believed for a long time that the circle of confession needs to be limited to the circle of offense. The issue here was that he was in a leadership role and had been living a lie before his family and his church. The circle of confession needed to include the church family. I told him what I felt he needed to do: to ask for forgiveness from his wife and children, and then to confess to the church the next time we met. He was willing to do both.

The next Sunday we had planned a baptismal service at one of our church family's homes, followed by a barbeque dinner. At the end of our worship and baptismal time I announced to several visitors who had come to witness the baptism of friends that we needed to have a "family" meeting for those who were committed to this fellowship. They understood and focused on watching the children and starting the burgers. We gathered in the large living room, seated on couches and chairs and mostly on the floor. I shared a few brief thoughts about confession, repentance, forgiveness and restoring one who has fallen. Then I gave my brother time to share in simple terms what he had done. The reaction of the gathered "family" still causes tears to well up in my eyes today. Immediately, brothers began to come to him and offer forgiveness and acceptance. I could hear them say that except for God's grace they too could be where he was.

For several minutes there was a flow of the most genuine care and love that I had ever witnessed. The ladies surrounded his wife, who sat in brokenness and shame, and they simply allowed the love of Christ to pour healing into her soul. I could never have imagined that something as difficult as this could have unfolded with such beauty and compassion. We made a commitment together that this was a "family" issue and that we would not gossip about it to anyone. We began to see our values emerging in the process of a real-life issue. We were committed to truth and modeling godliness, mercy and grace, restoration and restitution, and long-term relationships.

The preliminary hearing that was held left us all with a huge decision to make. If he paid the court an amount of money equal to the actual losses of his employer after insurance coverage, he would be placed in a minimum security prison just outside of our city with opportunity to see his family almost daily. If he did not pay, he would be sent to a state prison many hours away. The funds he had stolen were long spent. It was a Sunday morning after church when I shared this dilemma with the heads of households. Tuesday at noon was the deadline. Our little fellowship had little money to give towards this settlement. We shared the need, prayed and committed to seeking God for the part we could each play.

By late Tuesday morning, every dollar (nearly $10,000) had come from our little band of followers. We were able to "ransom" our brother and his family from months of separation and pain. He was able to work during this time, seeing his family daily while spending nights at the prison farm. He wrote a beautiful song during this time, the chorus of which simply says, "Everybody who belongs to Jesus, belongs to everybody who belongs to Jesus." I think that about sums up what God was teaching us!

Our dear friends Wally and Norma Wenge had come into our area to fulfill a calling of a "Joseph" kind of ministry, gathering excess fruit and vegetables to feed to the poor around the world. Our little band of brothers and sisters became the first team to process fruit in the village of Yettem (Armenian for 'Garden of Eden') that was dried and used to feed the hungry. Eventually they were able to purchase an old packing shed with ten acres and Gleanings For The Hungry was birthed. Wally and I spent many hours bending conduit and pulling wires, removing equipment from defunct food processing plants and fellowshipping around a common heart for mercy ministry. At one point in time, Willy and Diane returned to lead a Discipleship Training School at Gleanings. Most of the staff and the transient multitude of volunteer workers attended our church. This connection was a constant reminder to us of how practical faith reaches out to the poor and hungry and needy.

Under Pastor Steve's leadership, the whole church participated in a series of "Work Sundays". We gathered for a time of worship, all clad in coveralls and other work clothes. After worship we all headed out in different directions to mow lawns, paint fences, fix broken things and pull weeds for folks who were too sick, too old or too broken to do it themselves. A list had been compiled of needs in our neighborhoods so that folks knew we were coming to help them. These were wonderful times of fellowship for the entire family. Our children and youth were always excited about practicing their faith. We felt alive, and many were overwhelmed that we would come to serve them in this way. Occasionally we heard of someone who thought it was quite unspiritual to do such things on a Sunday… echoes of the criticism that Jesus received for healing on the Sabbath!

In the early 1990's we were invited to become part of the Foursquare Gospel Church. Their local church had experienced some difficult years and was about to be closed. I had developed a wonderful friendship with Pastor Roger Whitlow at Valley Christian Center in Fresno, and he had approached us about joining his tribe. The elders agreed unanimously that this was right and we became Wellspring Christian Center Foursquare Church.

One of the issues that arose was how do we deal with membership. I had some pretty strong opinions on the subject from years of seeing abuses and what I considered to be unbiblical ideas about the meaning of membership. I had acquired an old document titled Covenant of Fellowship. I don't remember the source, but I think it was an old English text. I studied the content and wrote my own text from my understanding of scripture. This became our "membership" document:

Covenant of Fellowship

Having been convicted by the Holy Spirit to confess and repent of my sin, and having surrendered the throne of my life to the Lord Jesus Christ as my Savior and Lord; and Desiring to share in the discipleship, worship, fellowship, and outreach of that portion of Christ's spiritual Body known as Wellspring Christian Center Foursquare Church; and Being in full agreement with and promising my support of this Body as governed by the elders under God,

I/We, _____ express my/our desire to enter into the following covenant with the brothers and sisters of this fellowship.

By the help and guidance of the Holy Spirit, who is our Helper and Comforter, we covenant:

To walk together in Christian love. (1John 3:14)

To care for and watch over one another. (Galatians 6:10)

To pray with and for one another, sharing our burdens, sorrows and joys. (Galatians 6:2; James 5:16)

To be thoughtful and courteous with one another, to be slow to take offense, and quick to forgive and seek forgiveness. (Ephesians 4:31-32)

To guard the scriptural purity, peace, and unity of this Body, and encourage its growth in Biblical knowledge and the application of scripture to life, (Ephesians 4:11-16; 1Timothy 4:12-16; 6:3-5; Jude 3)

To assist as the Lord enables and directs, in the work of the gospel on a personal level as well as through the various outreaches of this Body. (John 15:8,16; 20:21)

To contribute to the financial support of this ministry, and as the Lord directs and enables, to the relief of the needy and the evangelization of the lost. (2Corinthians 9:6-15; 1Corinthians16:1-2; James 1:27; Hebrews 13:2-3; Matthew 6:19-21)

To establish a regular quiet time for Bible reading and prayer, and whenever possible to establish family devotions in the home. (Psalms 119:97-105; Acts 17:11; 1Timothy 5:8)

To encourage and train the children that God has entrusted to our care, through the Word, consistent Godly discipline and personal example, so that they might know, love, and honor our God, and respect authority. (Ephesians 6:1-4; Colossians 3:20-21; 2Timothy 3:14-17; Proverbs 22:6,15; 29:15,17)

To be alert to the godless philosophies of this world, and to live an honest, upright, public and private life, being faithful to God's Word and diligent in its application to my lifestyle. (1Peter 2:11-16; Colossians 2:6-10; 2Timothy 2:8-6; 1John 3:7,10)

To call sinners to repentance and to the Lordship of Jesus Christ by example, by word, and by prayer. (John 4:35-38; Romans 10:1)

To regularly pray for those in positions of leadership and responsibility, and willingly submit to the Godly discipline and instruction of the elders who maintain loving oversight of this Body. (Hebrews 13:7; Titus 1:7-9)

To love and pray for all true believers and especially the suffering church. (Ephesians 6:18; Matthew 25.35-40).

The idea of transferring membership from our church to another had very little to do with a membership certificate or letter of reference, and had a great deal to do with making a new covenant with a new group of people to whom you would make a new commitment. This idea made it possible to apply our other teachings to membership.

Through the process of being involved in ministry and my personal study of gifts and ministries in scripture, I had come to realize some important things about myself. Even though the primary leader in most western churches is called "pastor", I knew very well that the gift of "pastor" was not my primary calling. I loved to start new things, was passionate about teaching, and was in my element when I was with other leaders who desired to grow in their faith. Much of my focus was outside the local church that I pastored.

It was time for our leadership team to get away for a time of refocusing. We headed up into the mountains to a cabin in the village of Wilsonia which was a private zone within the General Grant National Park. I presented the elders with a brief review of the many months of teaching I had done on gifts and ministries. I then handed out blank sheets of paper to everyone. We wrote the name of each person in the group on a separate sheet. I instructed them to go out and find a quiet place and to write in as much detail as possible, a description of each elder's ministry and gifts, ending with a description of themselves. Off we went into the hills! What followed was a divine moment for all of us!

After several hours apart, we gathered back together and began to share our writings. We each read what we had written about one of the guys and then had him read what he had written about himself. This continued around the room until all five of us had shared. We were exhilarated, encouraged, affirmed and accepted. I was astonished that each brother had in his own words identified the things that I understood about myself. I was not primarily a pastor by gift, but rather a teacher and leader, called to start new things and relate to the broader Body of Christ, not just one local church. Two brothers were strongly affirmed in their pastoral gifts, another as an administrator, and another as an evangelist. We returned to the valley with an awareness that we had participated in something very special and life-changing.

On Sunday morning with the elders all standing behind me on the platform, I related our experience to the church. For the first time I was able to fully express the tension I had felt between who I really was and what I thought was expected of me in a pastoral role. I was also able to publicly recognize the gifts of my brothers and bless the further release of those gifts within the church. I not only recognized their unique gifts, but publicly shared how I thought they might be more involved in the ongoing ministry of the church in the future. This was great fun!

One of my greatest joys at Wellspring was the constantly growing number of maturing leaders. I could go away on vacation and call upon a dozen different people to speak and know with confidence that they would prepare and present something very meaningful and valuable to the church. Our eldership couples enjoyed being together. We were friends first, leadership team members second.

Long-term relationships are born out of valuing people as people rather than seeing them as potential workers in the church. Community provides the sense of family that an institutional, business model cannot. Years after moving on from there, Ellie and I still consider these people to be among our dearest friends.

Let me share a few of the lessons we learned in the process of birthing this new work. Sometimes starting from the very beginning is the only way that you can continue in ministry. Even humble beginnings are non-the-less beginnings. Revisiting your values and reason for existence should be a regular exercise for leaders. Don't spoil the possibility of spontaneity by pre-planning everything. Influence can be disproportionate to numerical size. Investing in emerging leaders pays huge long-term dividends. Risk-taking needs to be re-introduced into our walk of faith. Transparency in leadership breeds honesty in followers. Connecting with the whole church in your community in a spirit of devotion to unity will be blessed by God!

PART TWO: Are We There Yet, Dad?

*The shortest distance between any two points
may be a straight line…
but life has few such lines!*
DH

*We cannot banish dangers,
but we can banish fears.
We must not demean life
by standing in awe of death.*
David Sarnoff

*Some people are so afraid to die
that they never begin to live.*
Henry Van Dyke

TEN:

Family Ties

*If a man does not know
how to manage his own household,
how will he take care of the church of God?*
1 Timothy 3:5 NASB

*My busyness and captivation with ministry success
had caused me to disconnect
from my own family.*
DH

God first... Family second... Ministry third! I had been taught this formula in Bible College and had taught it to others for several years. So why was I seeing such pain in my wife's eyes? Why was I feeling that ministry was against my family? I had worked extremely hard to develop a meaningful youth ministry with a rapidly growing group of kids. In less than two years our attendance had gone from fifteen to one-hundred and twenty-five. I had remodeled the youth chapel, installed a basketball court in the parking lot, and had youth activities several times a week. I directed two choirs and led in worship on Sunday. I tried to occasionally take a day off; but there was always something else to do for the church. I came home one day and noticed that my little daughter, Rachel was doing something that I had never seen before. I excitedly called Ellie so she could enjoy this new development too. Reality struck when she pointed out that Rachel had been doing this for quite some time and that I had simply not been there to see it.

My busyness and captivation with ministry success had caused me to disconnect from my own family. I had married the church! Ministry was my number one priority, God took second and family was a distant third place finisher. I had created an environment filled with weighty expectations. Cutting back on the things that I was now expected to do seemed impossible. I needed to revamp my values and priorities. The next Tuesday morning, I handed in my letter of resignation to the pastor. I needed a fresh start, a new devotion to my own household. This was a significant decision.

I wish I could tell you that I learned my lesson and that we rode off happily into the sunset filled with marital and family bliss. The truth is that tests like this repeat themselves throughout the years of ministry. The pressure of caring for the souls of women and men sometimes leads us to violate even the most sacred values that we have established.

We had now pioneered a church and it was growing in numbers and weight of responsibility. I had a very busy schedule both as senior pastor and chairman of the local ministerial association. My weekly planner was filled with appointments. One day, Ellie came by the office to see me and as usual I was in the middle of a counseling session. In a kind but direct manner she simply asked me if she could get on my schedule. I knew immediately that I was about to take another lap around the priority track that I thought I had mastered. I made two decisions that day that helped to reset my values. I informed my secretary that if my wife or daughters phoned the office or came by the office, regardless of what I was doing, she was to interrupt and let me know that they needed to talk to me. Secondly, I scheduled Ellie into my planner. I know this sounds less than romantic or spontaneous, but if you don't plan for something it usually doesn't just happen on its own. I set aside every Friday evening as our date night. If someone called and needed to meet that night, I would simply say that I was already booked. Now, there were times when an emergency interrupted our plans, and times when a wedding rehearsal needed to take place on that night, but generally it was only available to Ellie.

I learned quickly that those times were unique for us. We were able to move quickly from chatter about doing the business of life, into heart talk about how each of us was dealing with the reality of living life. Sometimes we went out to eat or went to a movie. Other times we licked ice cream cones sitting on the curb or walked nature paths. The place and activity was simply the backdrop to the main event: the lives of two people in love intersecting on the stage of life. We are in our thirty-eighth year of hanging out together, and it didn't just happen by accident!

I have also learned to value the perspective that Ellie brings to decisions that we need to make. There have been too many times that I have had to repeat to myself, "I should have listened to Ellie!" She has this uncanny ability (gift) to sense that something is a certain way without going through the normal process of weighing out the pros and cons and making lists of the benefits or drawbacks, and otherwise following my method of needing to think through every possible scenario that we might encounter. Why did God make us so different from each other? Oh! Yes! Opposites attract. If we were both the same one of us would be unneeded! But, I still should have listened to Ellie!

How many times on road trips did I refuse Ellie's suggestion to stop and ask for directions? How much time was wasted taking scenic routes when any gas station attendant could have directed us to a shorter way? Was our timing for returning to Canada to minister right for our youngest daughter, Sarah, who was left trying to finish high school without her parents? Was my unhappiness as a youth pastor in California linked to Ellie's initial lack of peace about accepting that role? Should I have written this book several years ago when she felt that it was my time to do so? Sadly, I must confess that I have missed some very important insights because of the times that I should have listened to Ellie... but didn't!

ELEVEN:

Survival

*I will never desert you,
nor will I ever forsake you.*
Hebrews 13:5 NASB

*The peanut butter eventually ran out,
but our faith in a God who is always
there for us never faded.*
DH

I asked Ellie how long she thought we could survive if I resigned from my very unhappy role as a youth pastor. Her response was a more limited timeline than I had in mind, but I was futuristic and faith-filled and naïve and impractical. Honest confession feels so good!

The local grocer agreed to order an extra case of Laura Scudder's Old-Fashioned Peanut Butter and sell it to us at a discounted price. Then there was the need for bread. We visited a health food store one day and discovered a well-built, high-priced Mill-n-Mix wheat grinder machine. I carefully dismantled part of it while Ellie kept the clerk busy, and decided that I could build one myself. The only truly proprietary parts were the grindstones and motor mounting ring. I asked the clerk if *replacement* stones were available, and after looking through her catalogue she announced that they were twenty-five dollars. To her surprise I ordered a pair. I assembled my version of the grinder over the next few days.

There was a wheat farmer nearby who was about to harvest his crop, who agreed to sell some to me. I borrowed a pickup, bought two fifty-five gallon steel drums and headed out to the field. The farmer filled the drums to the top straight out of the combine and off I headed, laughing about our good fortune. In the next months and years we ate whole-wheat cereal and pancakes and bread and birthday cakes and just about anything you could conceive of making with fresh-ground whole-wheat flour. The peanut butter eventually ran out, but our faith in a God who is always there never faded.

I have met so many pastor friends who are barely surviving "in the ministry", due to small congregations or small-hearted people or church histories laden with painful conflicts between former pastors and the congregation. My heart hurts for those who sincerely lay down their lives to care for a group of people, who are either unable or unwilling to provide a livable salary for them. Many pastors are bi-vocational, trying to work a full-time "secular" job while devoting "full-time" to pastoring a church.

Ministry is about far more than just trying to survive. It is about calling and passion and devotion. It happens whether or not we are paid for doing it. It is what we are created to do and we cannot not be doing it. We have a responsibility to our families to provide their basic needs. If the "work of the ministry" is not an adequate source to meet those needs, then we must actively pursue other sources. Ministry is not about living a certain economic lifestyle, nor about gaining recognition from position, but is about our passionate desire to serve God with our whole heart, using the gifts that He has planted within us.

The time of survival that I described above was an important re-evaluation time in my ministry life. Would I continue being the minister that God created me to be, even if I was not in an official ministry position with an official ministry salary? It was a time to refine my understanding of ministry and calling, to broaden my definitions into better alignment with God's idea of ministry.

TWELVE:

Death and Dying

Even though I walk through the valley
of the shadow of death,
I fear no evil;
for Thou art with me.
Psalm 23:4 NASB

Why have we institutionalized our feelings
and left ourselves to grieve alone
behind closed doors?
DH

I was only nine years old when baby Esther died, yet the loss of my little sister deeply affected my awareness of life and death. How could a beautiful young life come to such a sudden end? How was I as a child supposed to deal with the words of my mother who announced that morning that Esther had gone "to heaven" to be with Jesus. Why did she get to go and I had to stay behind? I was told that I would get to see her again if I went to heaven some day. Yet, in the midst of the questions and the attempted answers, there remained the deep hurting pain of loss.

I had experienced the traumatic death of my pet hamster, who had escaped the hand-crafted home that I had fabricated for him, and had eaten rat poison in Mrs. Hollingsworth's basement. I had watched and listened in horror as my dad decapitated chickens for our next month's meals, marveling at their ability to flap around, headless in the snow, leaving a crimson trail to mark their final journey. I was moved with compassion as I watched a tiny chipmunk writhing in its final moments of life, wondering to myself why I had chosen to shoot at it with my Daisy pellet gun. I had mercifully ended the life of a snake that had been run over by a car and was left pinned to the pavement with no hope of escape.

So, I was aware even as a child that a cycle of birth, life and death continued constantly around me, but this was different, this was my sister, a human being. There was a "sting" to death. There was the sudden absence of a baby who could no longer be held and pampered. There was the unanswered question, the why question that haunted me. There was the uneasy silence among family and church members that seemed to build a wall against any attempt to talk of death and dying. We didn't know how to deal with it, so we simply tried to move on with the business of living, without ever really dealing with the business of dying.

Looking back, I wonder how my parents were able to walk through this loss, yet continue to care for us without burdening us with the weight of their grief. Some clues can be found in an article that my mother wrote in the May 1968 issue of The Pentecostal Testimony, a newsmagazine of the Pentecostal Assemblies of Canada. That month's issue was devoted to mothers, and her article was entitled: "We Lost... Yet Found Again". She wrote:

> *"In everything give thanks, for this is the will of God in Christ Jesus concerning you." I have had a great deal to thank God for in my life, but a few years*

ago I was called upon to go through an experience that made me ask my Lord how I could give thanks when my heart was breaking.

The word of Paul in this scripture was a plea for steadfastness and I proved that I could be steadfast in the darkest hour, and look up and say, "Thank you dear Lord. I know that Thou doest all things well."

I believe I knew from the moment I carried my tiny eight month old daughter into the children's ward at our local hospital, and watched as the nurse replaced the little pink sleepers for a hospital gown, that I had held my baby for the last time on this earth.

MOTHER'S PREMONITION

Was it that I watched her become increasingly ill during the past three days after an attack of bronchitis that made me have this strange foreboding, or could it be a mother's premonition in such a crisis?

With a last glance at the still form in the small crib, I left with my husband for home. As cheerfully as possible we talked to our four older children as they prepared for bed. As each in turn said their prayers that night and remembered their little, sick sister in the hospital, I could only breathe, "Thy will be done."

Long hours after the children were peacefully sleeping and my husband had gone to get some rest, I opened the Book of all books where one finds wisdom, solace and comfort. As I read the great inspired pages I found that even in the shadow of death, the Almighty will not forsake.

The next thirty-six hours went by swiftly and yet each one seemed an eternity. Our little babe grew more ill until our family physician had to tell us *nothing more could be done for her. And so it was, in the night, her little heart could stand no more and she was absent from all suffering forever.*

PARENTS' CHALLENGE

Here, indeed, was a challenge for me as a mother of four other young children. The attitude I would take, and the impression those children would get from their Mommy and Daddy towards losing a loved one would remain with them through all their years.

I set about doing what I believe is the parents' duty to their children in the face of sorrow and crisis.

In her childhood, a friend's family had gone through a similar experience. Not even to the day she told me, could she forget the utter despair and gloom that settled over the entire household. It haunted her down through the years until she was frightened at the very mention of death. This I purposed in my heart should not happen to my children.

As they arose in the morning I told them the sad news. I will not soon forget the quick, enquiring, searching look each one gave me. As they saw the smile on Mother's face that always greeted them in the morning, I am certain their young, sorrowful hearts did not race so fast, nor did they think all enjoyment and laughter had ended, as if I had met them in tears.

As days went by our children never did see my husband or me weeping. We strove to be calm and outwardly cheerful each day and in the solitude and privacy of our own room – many times long hours into the night – we shed tears and released our grief.

THE CHILDREN RESPOND

We explained to our children that the body of their little sister must be laid beneath the ground, but her true, living self known as her soul, had taken its departure and gone back to its Maker in heaven. That is a number of years ago. Many times we have all gone up to the cemetery to tenderly care for the tiny grave. The children know in their hearts – and often say – that beneath the clay there lies the little "house" in which their sister lived on earth, but she is still alive in a fairer land.

NEW JOY

I yearned for my empty arms to be filled again and was overjoyed to realize we would be blessed with another child. I prayed earnestly that this one would also be a little girl and I believed my prayer would be answered.

Exactly a year after we buried our darling, little girl, my joy knew no bounds when I heard the doctor say to the attending nurse, "It's a girl...just what they wanted!"

God answered my prayer for which I humbly thank Him every day. She had not taken little Esther's place. No one could ever do that. But, she had filled a mother's deep longing and became the apple of her eye. The little sister that was taken is our guiding light to the Land above the blue.

SAME GUIDANCE FOR OTHERS

Many of my readers have been through a similar dark experience; many more may be called upon to travel such a road. Remember that God gives grace for each day.

Sorrow and grief are hard. The sting of death is cruel. But, we can and I say must, as parents, implant in the hearts of our children that even the shadow of death cannot hide God's face from us. Through the valley experiences we can rise to become stronger in character and more gentle and sympathetic to others.

I pray that I shall never have to tread the same dark path again, but I know there is strength and grace from above to meet the challenge. I am not sorry today that I met the crisis with calmness. Because of it, my husband and children and I rose to a higher understanding of the meaning of the scripture verse, "Yea, though I walk through the valley of the shadow of death, I will fear no evil, for Thou art with me." - Enid Hagey

I am so grateful that I had Godly parents who devoted themselves to helping me through this most difficult of my childhood experiences. As an adult, I feel the pain of their need to conceal how they really felt and how they really suffered alone. I wish I could somehow return to those days, bringing what I know from the present, to help them walk through this tragedy with the support they deserved. It just doesn't seem right that followers of Jesus should have to suffer the pain of grief alone.

Just twelve years later in 1980, I flew home from California, hoping to see my mom one more time. As I met my dad at the airport in Toronto, he gave me the sad news that she had gone "home" while I was traveling. My heart was pierced with deep loss. She had suffered for several years after undergoing neurosurgery for a brain tumor that left her partially paralyzed and unable to speak. This godly woman who had been at the center of our lives, the loudest cheerleader for our accomplishments, the gentle, deep strength in our times of turmoil, was gone.

She had seemed so perfectly normal in the Fall of 1972 when Ellie, our eight-month old daughter Tonya and I left Canada for adventure in California. A few short months later she had become a prisoner in her own changed body, unable to communicate the things that we knew she felt so deeply towards us and her circumstance. The voice of encouragement and support that I had grown to rely on and need in my life was silenced by paralysis.

Several years passed with her condition unchanged, interspersed with brief moments of hopeful faith for her healing. At one point in time, Ellie and I had become exposed to the "word of faith" or "positive confession" movement. We had convinced ourselves that if we did certain things, God would respond by healing my mother. We wrote to our family members and pressured them to join us in fasting and prayer so that when we gathered at Christmas, mom would be healed. Our attempts to move God's hand on her behalf failed, at least from our perspective. Our conclusion was that we had somehow not generated enough of whatever it was that God required from us.

There were no sufficient answers to our questions about "why" this happened to this wonderful lady. Sickness has a way of bringing us to the end of ourselves, to the end of simplistic formulas that sound good on paper, but are useless in the real world of pain and suffering. Sickness also brings us back from the far country of our wanderings and confronts us with the greater reality of eternity. Life is precious, its value beyond any of our other possessions.

On the day she died, as I walked through the airport on the way to the parking garage, I was suddenly aware of the presence of a loving, compassionate God. Deep within, I heard these words, "Your mom has joined the cloud of many witnesses! Run the race as if she is cheering for you from the stands!" The immediate pain of loss was interrupted with this amazing picture of comfort and hope and future. I later recalled the words from scripture that said:

> *Therefore, since we have so great a cloud of witnesses surrounding us, let us also lay aside every encumbrance, and the sin which so easily entangles us, and let us run with endurance the race that is set before us, fixing our eyes on Jesus, the author and perfecter of faith, who for the joy set before Him endured the cross, despising the shame, and has sat down at the right hand of the throne of God. Heb 12:1-2 NASB*

And there she was... my mother, cheering in the stands, able not only to speak, but to again encourage and challenge me in my own journey home.

A few hours later I wrote these words of tribute that were shared at her memorial service (I realized as I wrote them here that they so closely parallel the words I wrote at the death of her brother, my Uncle Eric. They were of similar heart!):

> *We have watched and listened in amazement at the vastness of the circle of our precious mother's influence, as friends and neighbors from near and far away have come to share this time with us. It seems not to matter whether these ones have come from times of knowing mom from years ago or only weeks ago – whether from times of joy or deep sorrow – whether from small towns where she once found her abode, or even the small room, her home until so few days ago – for all have in their words and ways confirmed again: the worth, the beauty, the simple quiet gentleness that was our mom.*

Their words even now ring so clearly in our ears:

"Enid was a very special person."

"Enid was a real inspiration to me."

"Enid was such a beautiful person."

"It was Enid who helped me make it through the death of my little boy."

"Enid expressed through her life the fruit of the spirit more than anyone else I have ever known."

To those many whose lives were made richer by her simple gift of herself, she was so much like a beautiful, strong tree bearing an abundant supply of the choicest fruit for all in need to pick freely. A tree stands quietly doing that which is most natural for it to do – bear fruit. Mom gave so much in her short life-time, yet so quietly, so kindly, so much like a tree doing what is most natural… bearing fruit.

What was that fruit?

There was a deep LOVE for all that God has made, a heart of warmth, caring always with unselfish care for those in need of love.

A life of JOY was hers, fun-loving, enjoying simple things that others may have missed. Her joy brought happiness in times that otherwise were hard and rough.

She lived at PEACE with herself, her God, her family and all those who passed her way. When baby Esther died, so small, she wrote these words from her heart at peace with God:

"Oh! Blessed Lord, I love Thee more, through
  all my grief and pain.
I know that Thou doest all things well, through
  sorrow I shall gain.

I asked Thee Lord if 'twas Thy will, that Thou wouldst make her well,
And Thou didst answer, 'twas Thy plan, with Thee she went to dwell.
Oh Lord, please give me courage, to live from day to day,
And sometime I will understand, just why she went away.
Use me, as Thou seest best, to do my part for Thee,
That Thou might hasten Thy return. Oh! Then my babe I'll see."

And we as normal children often picked the fruit of PATIENCE which was so very much a part of our dear mother's life.

Her KINDNESS and GOODNESS could simply be described with this one little illustration: A little ninety year-old lady lived next door when we were all small children. Every evening at suppertime mom would disappear briefly, then return to feed us. Without fanfare or boasting she would daily feed the little, lonely lady with a hot, nourishing meal. Our Master's words so clearly fit that extra plate she filled, when Jesus said, "If you have done it unto one of these little ones, you have done it unto Me."

FAITHFULNESS was also hers, to the family, to her husband, her God, her church; always there, available, never even able to take a job outside the home for more than a week or two because it interfered with her real mission and calling as a wife and mother and friend.

And yes, she was full of GENTLENESS and SELF-CONTROL, even when faced with critical *neural-surgery, she was strong, trusting God and encouraging all of those around her.*

And, like a tree, we look not upon the great trunk or branches, the limbs or leaves... we look upon the fruit. In remembering our dear mother, the fruit is overwhelming, the harvest has just begun, for it is the kind of fruit which will remain.

Solomon described this jewel from God in Proverbs 31, and we join with him and say, "We, her children, do rise up and call her blessed!"

The memorial service was typically nice with the usual readings and preaching being directed at the yet unconverted among us. But, the weighty things of remembrance came before and after the official service from the honest and sincere storytelling of so many of the guests who came to grieve with us. We don't do well at grieving in North America. We have so sanitized death and its aftermath that we have forgotten how to "weep with those who weep."

I worked at a funeral home for a few months before we went with YWAM to Europe. I was amazed at all of the preparations for the viewing. Hairdressers came in to wash and blow-dry the hair of the deceased. Make-up artists spread thick layers of rouge, eye-shadow and powder. Eyeglasses were positioned just right. The finest clothes were placed on the body before it was laid in a wooden or metal box lined with colored fabric.

I was confused by the comments of some of the viewers as they remarked at how good mom looked lying there. The truth was that she was dead! She had experienced long-term pain and suffering. She was often frustrated by the disabilities that her sickness had placed upon her. She was gone from us, no longer present in our lives. It hurt deeply to lose her, then to experience a cosmetically-correct, sterile response to her passing. Why can't we just be real?

I am so grateful for those who do understand how to grieve, who are not afraid to simply shed authentic tears in your presence, who themselves have lost the precious bonds of earthly connection and have not forgotten the lessons of their experience.

The Apostle Paul wrote about this shared comfort when he said:

Blessed be the God and Father of our Lord Jesus Christ, the Father of mercies and God of all comfort; who comforts us in all our affliction so that we may be able to comfort those who are in any affliction with the comfort which we ourselves are comforted by God. 2 Corinthians 1: 3-4 NASB

I wonder if Job in the midst of his great personal losses experienced the same need for a genuine response from his peers. He said:

*I go about mourning without comfort;
I stand up in the assembly and cry out for help.* Job 30:28 NASB

My dad was a hard-working building contractor of Swiss-German descent. His Mennonite roots could be traced back seven generations to Hans Jacob Hagey in Switzerland. He was a no-nonsense, meat-and-potato kind of man, who expressed his love for us through providing for our needs. He was not given to many physical or verbal displays of affection.

I have a file filled with every one of my report cards, and they were all signed by my mother. That signature was assurance to the teacher that parents had actually seen and reviewed the grades. It wasn't that dad didn't care about our progress in school as children, he simply felt that certain things were women's work and other things were for the men. This of course was subject to some variation if our grades started to slip downward!

I grew up longing for the approval of my dad. I wanted to know from a masculine source that I was doing alright, that I was moving in the right direction to become a man myself someday. I worked for him from the time I was about eight; I spent time mixing and transporting mortar up extension ladders and onto home-made wooden scaffolding, along with my older brother, Howard. During high school and college years I worked with dad building huge chicken barns for the Shaver Poultry Breeding Company that had become his exclusive employer. All the while, I was hoping to hear words of approval for my work, affirmation that I was becoming manly, acceptance into the club of the masculine. Dad expected good work, really nothing short of excellence. He had often told us that if a job was worth doing, it was worth doing right and only once. His comments about my work usually consisted of correcting or critiquing something that didn't quite meet the mark, rather than congratulating me for doing it right.

I moved to California in 1972 and after a dozen or so years had decided to design and build a home for my family. This part-time project took about four years to complete. In 1988 I was getting down to the final touches including building the kitchen cabinets. I don't know how much of this was subconscious, and how much was based upon my overt need for approval, but I called dad and asked if he could come down and help with the finish work. Swiss-German clockmakers in your family tree somehow passed on the penchant for details and precision; I wanted the cabinets to look good. But, I wanted something much deeper to happen. I wanted this grandest project of my life to be the catalyst for the uncorking of a lifetime of deferred approval from dad. I knew that I had the skills to complete the finish work by myself, but I needed him to bring approval, affirmation and acceptance.

The early morning phone call from my younger brother Barry carried with it far more pain and despair than the words themselves conveyed. Dad had been found dead of a massive heart attack at the site of a cabin he was building for a neighbor at Braeside Christian Camp.

He wasn't coming to approve my work! He was gone and I could do nothing about it! Something died within me that day.

April 30, 1988 was my fortieth birthday and the day I laid my dad to rest. It doesn't seem to matter how old you are, for in the presence of your parents you are still their boy or girl, a child in a grown-up body. That day, I realized that I had become the older generation in my family. My parents were gone, and in so many ways the "buck" now stopped with me. I guess I had become a man without participating in any "rite of passage" or consenting to any prescribed list of responsibilities.

I wrote these words as a tribute to dad; they were read at his funeral:

> *Is he the head of household affairs to whom*
> *We look for strength, stability and that special*
> *Sense of security – just because he is there?*
> *Is he the man of work who leaves early in*
> *The morning – returning late, weary, yet*
> *Satisfied that a day's work well-rendered*
> *Will provide the food, the clothes, the shelter –*
> *The things of life to keep the family*
> *Warmed and clothed and fed?*
> *Is he the voice and hand of discipline,*
> *Heeded quickly – without doubting his intentions*
> *To produce not only changed behavior but*
> *Long-term Godly character?*

*Is he the model – copied by sons, who in
The struggle of maturing, look for clues
In how to be a man? Yet gentle,
Moved in heart, compassionate, a friend?
Is he the man of counsel whose practical
Advice demands consideration through future
Years of life?
Oh! Yes! The answer is all of these and more.
Our Dad who loved us deeply, provided faithfully,
Disciplined, directed us, let us know he cared!
If we can work with diligence in what we're
Called to do – we know, Dear Dad, that this will
Be attributed to you.*

It was six weeks before I found the strength of mind and heart to re-enter the building project. I stood in our unfinished home, weighted down with the hopelessness that had befallen me the day of the phone call. In the midst of my complaint to God, I heard His gentle, kind, yet penetrating voice:

"Build it for Me as your heavenly Father!"

That day marked the beginning of a long-time process of discovering the beauty and wholeness of a new kind of relationship with my heavenly father.

I was awakened abruptly by one of those very early morning phone calls that always seem to carry intense news, either good or bad. It was July 28, 1982. A friend wanted to know if we had heard the tragic news of a plane crash in Texas that had killed Keith Green, his three year old son, Josiah, two year old daughter Bethany, another whole family and the pilot. Melody was home with one year old Rebekah, six weeks pregnant with their fourth child, Rachel. The local Christian radio station was broadcasting the news and devoting the entire day to his music. Over and over we heard his songs: *Your Love Broke Through, Asleep In The Light,*

There Is A Redeemer, So You Wanna Go Back To Egypt and many more. We were stunned and shocked!

Ellie and I were living in eastern Texas around the time that Keith and Melody had purchased land to relocate Last Days Ministries from Los Angeles. Keith's music was a constant favorite in our home, and we always looked forward to The Last Days Newsletter, a provocative and practical call to authentic faith. Keith was one of the most sincere, real, devoted followers of Jesus that we had ever encountered. He had said:

> *I repent of ever having recorded one single song, and ever having performed one concert, if my music, and more importantly, my life has not provoked you into Godly jealousy or to sell out more completely to Jesus!*
>
> *When I die I just want to be remembered as a Christian.*

I had felt a stirring in my soul over several years to write about my personal faith. When I started to receive Keith's newsletters, a subtle argument arose within my mind. Why should I write when they are doing such an amazing job of writing about some of the same subjects that impassioned me? This surrender on my part left me doing nothing more than living part of my calling through a surrogate. The day of the plane crash, God shook my soul. I was confronted with my years of excuses. I could no longer be excused.

I began to write a series of articles in a small newsletter called The Night Watchman. The first article that I wrote was titled, *A Watchman, Called To Make My Pen A Trumpet.* (The role of watchmen is described in the book of Ezekiel, chapters two and three). My friend Craig Meadors devoted his time to doing the layout and developing some wonderful graphics, including a sketch of me holding a pen, the tip of which had become a trumpet. I continued to write short articles from time to time, but the book in your hands is really the culmination of my years of wanting to be authentic in my faith. I am grateful to Keith for provoking me to greater faith.

We have so many relationships that have taught us about death and loss. We had gotten to know Les and Anita while on our whirlwind summer trip visiting churches in western Canada. We had heard of them and they of us, but this was our first actual meeting. It is one of the joys of our faith to meet brothers and sisters that we have heard about through others. They had been involved for several years with the King's Kids ministry of Youth With A Mission. At the time we met, they were well into the process of developing a cell-based church in the Dawson Creek, BC area. They were fun-loving and deeply passionate about their calling. It was one of those friendships that starts off as if it has already existed for years. It was quite a shock to get the news a few months later, that Les had developed intestinal cancer. We continued to connect with them, even visiting in a little motel near the Mexican border where they stayed while he received cancer treatments in Tijuana.

Months passed, and Les was in very serious condition. Ellie and I felt that it was time for us to head back up to Dawson Creek to be with them. We spent many hours of his last week just hanging out at his hospital bedside. During this time we were confronted by several believers who informed Anita that it was her lack of faith that was keeping Les from being healed. Why is it that at the point of our greatest need for support and kindness, we receive instead the judgment of Bible-quoting "saints" who apparently believe that they have superior insight into the meaning and solution to the heartbreak in which we find ourselves?

On Easter Sunday morning, with his room filled with family and friends singing songs of worship, Les slipped

In Search of the Church

quietly through the thin curtain that separates physical and eternal realities. He was gone from us, the husband, father, pastor and friend. The pain was real, the separation rending.

We decided to stay in Anita's basement apartment to help her and the church through this difficult time. What we thought might take a few weeks lasted a year and a half. This was a wonderful opportunity for us to walk through the process together of healing a broken wife, family and church.

Our daughter Rachel awaited the arrival of her dear friend, Charity. They had planned to spend the day together visiting bridal shops to find the perfect bridesmaid dresses for Charity's upcoming wedding. Then, tragedy struck! Charity was involved in a very serious traffic accident just south of town. Her head injuries were so severe that she died during the night. Rachel called me in the midst of her own pain and brokenness to give me the news. I was in the midst of packing up our little apartment in Abbotsford, to join Ellie in Dawson Creek to be with Anita during her loss.

Charity was a wonderful young lady, full of life and hope and talent. When we met in her parents' home as a leadership cell (several couples who had been involved in various ministries, who were now trying to discern their next step), she would sit with her guitar and lead us in sweet times of worship. She was fun to be around. She was amazingly simple in her love for Jesus and people.

We sat as a family at Wellspring Christian Center the Sunday after she died. I am so grateful to Pastor Willy for being sensitive to the many in attendance who were struggling to make any kind of sense out of this tragedy. Instead of the usual proceedings, he chose to allow us to grieve together, to share openly our thoughts and memories of this beautiful, young lady. At one point, Rachel's soul seemed to burst wide open with the stored-up pain of the previous few days.

Weeping is a doorway to a pathway of healing that no amount of words or advice or sermonizing could ever accomplish. Tears flowed unchecked that Sunday morning, people laid aside the dignity that accompanies the expected public response to death, and discovered the beauty of a church family weeping with those who weep. This was one of those times of revelation, of witnessing God's favor being poured upon people who were not afraid to humanize their faith.

I have included many details about the things I have felt and written during times of loss. I have done this because I believe that it is so important for us to be able to share in the process of grieving together. It is in my freedom to tell you about these parted loved ones that I find healing for my own pain. Why have we institutionalized our feelings and left ourselves to grieve alone behind closed doors like my parents dealing with the loss of baby Esther? It is almost like we have tried to reverse the incarnation. Jesus, who was fully divine, took on the form of humanity and was not "out of touch with our reality" (Hebrews 4:15, The Message). We, in our pursuit of the divine, have too often forgotten to be fully human. Death is a painful loss to us who must remain on the earth-bound side of the curtain. My friend, Pastor Barry, greeting a multitude of friends attending his dear wife's funeral, simply said to Ellie and me, "I don't know what I'm going to do without her." That is human! That is reality! Our clichéd words and actions will never bring the soothing and healing virtue of a sensitive human heart, itself touched by the unanswerable questions that surround death and dying.

Last night Ellie and I watched the fascinating PBS documentary, *A Family Undertaking*, that described the Home Funeral movement across the United States. Many families are keeping their departed loved one at home, caring for them with tenderness, preparing them for burial, decorating the casket, and walking through the grief process in the natural setting of their home as compared to the sterile, foreign setting of a funeral home. This decision is not primarily a financial one, but based upon a desire to participate more fully in the experience of bidding farewell to the ones that have shared the whole of their lives interconnected with our own. I find this to be very significant in the overall discussion of death and dying and the potential role of the church in this process. People are moving away from institutionalized services and toward more meaningful family-community involvement. Are we hearing what the world around us is saying?

I received this little story by email from a friend recently. It sums up with simplicity what I have tried to say here.

(Author and lecturer Leo Buscaglia once talked about a contest he was asked to judge. The purpose of the contest was to find the most caring child. The winner was a four year old child whose next door neighbor was an elderly gentleman who had recently lost his wife.)

> Upon seeing the man cry, the little boy went into the old gentleman's yard, climbed onto his lap, and just sat there. When his Mother asked what he had said to the neighbor, the little boy said, "Nothing, I just helped him cry."

THIRTEEN:

Burnout

Restore to me the joy of Thy salvation.
Psalm 51:12 NASB

*What is it about pastoring
that leads us to these points
of despairing for our own health
and family relationships?*
DH

I had resigned as senior pastor of Wellspring Christian Center. My dear friend and associate pastor Steve Witmer had become their new leader. For the next three years I faded deeply into obscurity, crawling away to find a place of healing and restoration from the weariness of years of pioneering a new ministry. I developed a growing sense of my own weakness and entertained thoughts that perhaps I might never again be involved in traditional ministry. I cringed when the phone rang, thinking that it might be a pastor needing me to speak during his vacation. I felt that I had nothing to say and no passion left with which to say it. I was a classic burned out clergyman.

In Search of the Church

Our local newspaper printed a weekend magazine insert called Parade. In the April 14, 1991 edition the front cover had a picture of an Episcopal Priest with this caption: *"When A Healer Needs Healing: Tens of thousands of America's clergy of all faiths find themselves burned out by the pressures of their calling – and the number is growing."* The article defines burnout as *"a disease of the overcommitted who refuse to come to terms with their limitations."*

One week later in the Metro section of the same newspaper I read this heading: *"Rock Fellowship ends operations after 12 years."* In the article that followed was this poignant comment from the pastor who was leaving, "Ministry burnout is possible for even the most dedicated. With concerns for our health and our marital stability we have after much prayer and soul searching made one of the most difficult decisions of our ministerial career."

What is it about pastoring that leads us to these points of despairing for our own health and family relationships? Is it an unrealistic view of ourselves and our roles? Is it the weight of expectations that we heap on ourselves and allow others to attach to us? Is it our demanding schedules that allow so little time to just stop and smell the roses?

A number of years ago Ministers Life Insurance Company of Minneapolis published a brochure called *"Clergy Stress and Burnout"*. A few of the key thoughts were:

> *A certain amount of stress or tension is necessary for renewal and growth. But too much – and too constant – stress can ruin your health and shorten your life. Thus, the question is not how to take all the stress out of ministry, but how to make stress manageable. Stress and threat of burnout "comes with the calling" in the ministry. Studies show that ministers most vulnerable to burnout are: idealistic and over-committed; have rigid standards for their role; are social activ-*

ists; are inclined to avoid conflict by trying to satisfy everybody; are in constant direct contact with the poor, dying, sick and hurting; suffer from role confusion; can't seem to protect their personal boundaries for rest, relationships and relaxation. After all, being constantly overstressed is not only destructive to the minister as a person; it is also contrary to the spirit of pastoral commitment. The minister's role is that of "one who serves." Constant overstress diminishes capacity to serve effectively. The pastor must stay well, not only for self and family, but also for the congregation's sake. As pastoral counselor Charles Rassieur puts it, in his book, **Stress Management for Ministers** *(1982, Westminster Press, Santa Ana, CA 92703):Pastors who consciously and without apology take good care of themselves have by far the best chance to be servants of Christ for all the years of their calling.*

The article then outlines a number of ways for a pastor to be revitalized. Finding fresh spiritual disciplines (new ways to pray and read scripture, daily meditation, personal retreats and silent contemplation, spiritual mentors). Taking time off (daily and weekly breaks, quarterly long weekends off, yearly breaks of a month, sabbaticals every six to eight years to renew and recharge). Establishing support networks (clergy peers, weekly prayers by the congregation for their pastor, encouragement from the denominational leadership). Enriching life at home (marriage enrichment events, giving the pastor and his family space to be a family). Getting regular exercise (frequent, regular, interesting exercise, planned to fit our temperament, schedule and resources, 30-60 minutes, at least three times a week). Practicing self-assessment (take time to assess your own needs and points of greatest stress, evaluate how you are coping with these needs and stress).

Getting therapy (honest admission of need can lead to new vitality and healthy ministry). Laughing (we need to learn to take ourselves less seriously and receive the healing power of laughter).

Ellie had noticed for quite some time that I found it very difficult to relax even during our family vacation times. On one trip we backpacked several miles with some of our gear on horses. Our youngest, Sarah, rode on an old horse named Choktah for part of the trek, hanging on tightly behind the heavy packs on its back. Crown Valley was a breathtaking destination and the old Dude Ranch, now owned by our friends and church members, the Johnsons, was a welcomed site after our journey. It was a perfect place to relax and enjoy the beauty of nature. Not for me! I was driven to design and plumb a heated shower stall made from the assorted leftovers of years of previous visits. I remember bragging about my MacGyverish abilities. The shower worked great. We all enjoyed at least a short warm shower during those few days, at the expense of my driven and weary mind and body and the frustration of my wife who wondered why I couldn't relax a little.

Shortly after our return down the mountain, Ellie gave me a wonderful gift. It was the book, **When I Relax I Feel Guilty** by Tim Hansel (1979, Chariot Family Publishers, Elgin, IL). The subtitle is, *"Discover the wonder and joy of really living."* I felt that she was trying to tell me something. My perceptive and sensitive Swiss German mind picked up on that. The book was a great help. I learned how important it is to take breaks in the midst of stressful situations; that vacations are not the only times to find rest and relaxation; that "micro" and "mini" vacations can add freshness to life and relationships. I decided that I would not be so driven, that I would be more aware of the harmful "adrenalin rush" syndrome that energized my long hours and days, that I would stop trying to gain approval from the workaholics in my life, that I would not feel guilty for relaxing. I actually started taking coffee breaks. When stress and pressure reached a high level in the office, I would go for a short walk and breathe deeply. Ellie and I took several "mini" vacations a year which usually consisted of an overnight stay in a mountain cabin owned by our friends the Kipers. Whenever we passed the five thousand foot elevation marker, which coincided with the incredible smell of the evergreens, I would feel a literal sense of peace and relaxation come over me. I was still driven at times, still struggled with my A.D.D., still had deadlines to meet and people-problems to resolve, but I had a plan to keep healthy.

It is so important that congregational leaders recognize the serious toll that long-term stress can take on their pastoral staff. Honesty on both sides can lead to a plan that benefits the pastor and his family as well as the church.

Pastors would never admit that at times we function under a "Messiah" complex. It is in our attempts to be the savior of every person and situation that we crash and burn. Our workload is heavy, the diverse expectations can be overwhelming, the "need to be needed" can create a vicious circle of activity and dependence, family demands and our perception of failing them can be weighty, feelings of being unappreciated for all that we do which often includes feeling underpaid for our investment can gnaw away at our self-esteem, and the congregation's expectation that the pastor has all of the answers to every situation places him or her on a shaky pedestal.

For the sake of pastors and churches let's get real with each other. Let's assess how we are doing. Let's make a plan that will keep our pastor from burnout and help them finish well.

FOURTEEN:

Renewal: Expired Shelf-Life

I am exceedingly afflicted;
Revive me, O LORD.
Psalm 119:107 NASB

Churches and individual followers of Christ
cannot function spiritually very long
without regular times of God's visitation.
DH

The three years of being *out of the ministry* because of burnout had been painful in many ways. We had been pretty much forgotten by most of those to whom and with whom we had ministered for the years before. Pastors who had been our peer friends weren't sure how to approach us in what appeared to them to be a failure to succeed under stress. Our circle of friends was narrowed down to the true friends who love us for who we are, not for our accomplishments. It is these kinds of events on our journey that help us to redefine the values of our lives. I suspect that we are not alone in this discovery.

Pastor Steve, now three years into his senior pastoral ministry, came by my home office one morning. Our friendship has been one of transparency and honest assessment. He described his own deep valley of spiritual dryness which had peaked publicly the previous Sunday. He stood to preach but was overwhelmed with his own need for more of God, and his inability to lead the church into a spiritual experience that he was not enjoying himself. He stopped mid-sermon and confessed his personal need for a revived spiritual life. When he asked the congregation if any of them were in the same condition, about eighty percent raised their hands. The service ended with a time of prayer as pastor and people asked God for something fresh in their lives.

As he sat in my office, exposing the painful heart of a broken shepherd, I could only respond from my own spiritual dryness. I had nothing to offer my best friend except a second-hand invitation to a renewal conference about to be held at the Anaheim Vineyard. Our daughter, Tonya, had been attending a Vineyard Fellowship in San Luis Obispo and had experienced firsthand a fresh touch of grace in her own life. She had purchased tickets for Ellie and I to attend this conference and had boldly informed us that God was about to take us off the shelf and do new things in our lives. We planned to attend, and I suggested that maybe Steve could join us. After all, what could be worse than our current state? He decided to sign up.

We arrived in Anaheim at the *"Let The Fire Fall: Renewing Your Passion For Jesus"* conference. The place was packed to the rafters. There was a tangible atmosphere of expectancy. It was noisy, at times downright crazy even by charismatic standards of decency. We saw things we had never witnessed before. We heard sounds that were strange. Steve was swept into a river of refreshing. He had become so spiritually intoxicated that he could barely walk, and was certainly in need of a designated driver back to the motel.

When he called his wife, Becky, she simply wanted to know if he would be "normal" upon his return. I observed all that was happening with the critical eye of a theologian, the concerned eye of one who didn't want to do anything foolish in a public setting, the cold heart of a man distant from God.

Toward the final hours I became desperate before God. "I don't care how it looks, how it feels, how it sounds, I just need You to touch me!" As I sat beside Ellie, she began to pray over me, simply, gently, compassionately. What happened next can only be described in a metaphor. Ocean waves started to crash over me, one after another. I was engulfed and overwhelmed in the love of God for me. I didn't want it to end. I had never been baptized in His love like this. I had always known that He loved me, but this was my first real experience of His love. It was dramatic, real, transforming and refreshing.

The next Sunday as Steve stood to tell of his time of refreshing, people began to run to the altar without invitation; renewal had begun at Wellspring.

A few months later we joined the Wellspring leadership team at the first year anniversary of God's visitation at the Toronto Airport Vineyard. Another step in my journey to health took place one evening as I lay on the floor in the huge hotel ballroom.

I want to repeat part of my story that was shared in Chapter 12, because it plays an important part in my renewal experience. The death of my father left me feeling that I had never received his approval and affirmation as a man. I knew that he had grown up in a generation that chose to withhold, or simply didn't know how to show or verbalize affection, but I had still tried very hard to earn that attention from him. When I received the phone call that he had died I was shocked and angry and heartbroken. He was never coming to affirm the little boy that still needed a father's approval.

God has an amazing ability to make sense out of the broken pieces of our souls. As I lay on the floor in Toronto, He spoke deeply into my wounded heart with words of restoration. He knew how painful my loss had been. He knew my need for a father's affirmation. The next revelation caught me a bit by surprise. I watched as my years of ministry passed before me: the sermons, the counseling, the evangelism programs, leadership in the ministerial association, camps, and on it went. I heard that familiar voice again, lovingly assuring me that I didn't need to "do" ministry to gain His approval. He asked me this piercing question, "How much would be enough to gain My approval?" I was stunned and humbled before Him. There was nothing I could do to gain His approval. Then I heard these kind and healing words, "Even if you never do another thing in ministry, I will still love you!" The waves of His love and acceptance and affirmation flowed over me again. I was being *fathered* by the best Dad in the universe. The weeks and months that followed were indeed times of being taken *off of the shelf* of obscurity. Ministry became fun and fulfilling. Doors opened in dozens of churches for us to tell of our journey and of God's wonderful grace.

Churches and individual followers of Christ cannot function spiritually very long without regular times of God's visitation. Some of those times may be dramatic like the Toronto Blessing, most are less spectacular, but still essential. Regularly scheduled personal renewal retreats for people in ministry are significant. A freshness of spirit in our leaders will affect the quality of ministry they provide. We all benefit!

FIFTEEN:

Return To Hockey-land

*For you have not as yet come to the resting place
and the inheritance
which the LORD your God is giving you.*
Deuteronomy 12:8-9 NASB

He chooses our inheritance for us.
Psalm 47:4 NASB

*Have you ever wondered if the "main event"
is really not the main event?*
Pastor Barry McGaffin 2007

When my dad died, I so desperately wanted to have something of his that would remind me of the life he had lived. When I got back to Paris, Ontario from California, I entered the cabin where he had spent his last moments. There on a saw-horse hung his nail apron with the hammer that he had swung so many thousands of times to drive nails through timber. I grabbed it and clutched it in my hands, so aware that his strong hand had gripped it just hours before. When my mom had died, dad remarried, and I knew that my "inheritance" was likely limited to what I held in my hands. I tucked the hammer away into the trunk of the rental car, like a little boy hiding a treasure under a rock. I still carry that hammer in my tool bag and each time I use it I am reminded of my birthright.

Ellie's dad had died a couple of years earlier and her experience had been similar. He had remarried after Ellie's mom died, and when he died, all of his possessions passed on to his second wife and her family. Ellie was able to sort through a few books and find a handful of keepsakes. She also acquired his old felt hat that he had worn so often to complete his gentlemanly attire.

There was a certain sadness that we both felt upon realizing that our inheritance had been passed on to others who had walked only the last few steps of our fathers' journeys. It wasn't so much the *cash value* of what could have been ours (although we certainly would have welcomed that blessing), as it was the feeling of having what was intended for us, taken by others. So, when God seemed to be leading us back to Canada in 1999, with a sense of restoring our inheritance to us, deep feelings were being revisited. Let me backtrack a little to fill in the process that led to the decision to return..

Having grown up in Canada, we both had a love for our *homeland* and for our people. Regardless of where our journey takes us, we carry in our hearts a connection with our roots. Our friends, the Andres, who left their home and land in Zimbabwe at a point of the tragic leadership failure of Mugabe, still talk fondly of their "nation" and their people.

Ellie and I had spent part of our twenty-fifth wedding anniversary in 1995 attending a "Gathering of the Nations" conference in Whistler, British Columbia. During that week, we began to see that God was doing some new things among our Canadian sisters and brothers that were dramatically different from what we had experienced before we left Canada in 1972. Where there had been deeply entrenched factions, we were witnessing the breaking down of dividing walls, the genuine love and acceptance of the whole church. Generational barriers seemed destined to crumble in this environment of affirmation and acceptance. There appeared to be a new awareness of the one church and a willingness to remove the man-made walls of divisive comparisons birthed by sectarian hearts. Hopefulness arose in our hearts that God was up to something, that His people were responding to His overtures.

During the next couple of years, following a time of personal, spiritual refreshing, we had made several trips from California to Western Canada to share our stories and encourage the churches. My friend Steve, had seen a visionary picture of fires being started in the towns and villages all along the highways of Western Canada. Several traveling teams ministered along those routes over the next number of months. People were hungry for a deeper connection with God, and we had the privilege of encouraging them in that pursuit.

Ellie and I had felt directed to take an entire summer to travel in British Columbia, Alberta and Saskatchewan (the three western provinces of Canada). The sense that we had was that God wanted to "show us the church." The scary and stretching part for me was that we felt that we were not to plan this trip out, but to follow God's daily leading to discover who we were to meet, where we were to stay and so on. As we drove north from California, we passed through the dairy country of Washington and at one point in time I looked out upon a huge feedlot with hundreds of cows all lined up eating their prepared feed. They were all facing away from me, so you can picture which portion of their anatomy was predominant. I clearly heard God speak into my heart, "This is what it looks like to Me when you always have to have all your ducks lined up in a row!" Ellie was asleep at the time, but I could hardly wait to tell her about

God's humorous, yet poignant affirmation of direction for how we were to approach our summer trip.

Our only scheduled contact was with the President of the Foursquare Churches in Canada. He graciously received us and invited us to visit a few of his pastors who he felt would be encouraged by us. We headed out on the road and into an adventure that was really quite amazing. We would visit a pastor and his family in a town or city, then they would connect us with someone further down the road that they thought needed encouragement, and on it went. We simply asked for an evening meal together and a place to sleep. On average it took about an hour and a half together before these precious leaders would begin to open their hearts to us, sharing their pain, frustration, doubts and marital stress. Most of our visits lasted into the early hours of the morning and ended with times of tearful prayers and re-birthed hope. After breakfast, we bid them farewell and drove on to the next divine appointment. By the end of forty-nine days on the road, we had spent quality time with forty-seven pastoral families, from thirteen different denominations in three different provinces. God was indeed showing us the church in Canada.

We knew that we were to return to our roots. Our home in California was up for sale, and we informed our circle of friends that we would be moving north as soon as the house sold. But, it didn't sell! And then it didn't sell some more! In the middle of this stretching, we seemed to constantly connect with people who had dramatic stories of how God sold their home for them. Stories began to be blown out of proportion for us. You know what I mean! One family had just thought about selling, when a man with a large briefcase came to the front door asking if they would be interested in selling their home for "cash", then insisted on paying more than their imagined asking price, and would cover all of their moving expenses. Everywhere we went, we heard similar stories of how the "cosmic real estate company" had sold homes so that people could go elsewhere to do God's will. What was wrong with us? Then, one day as I had just uttered the words to someone, "We will go to Canada when the house sells", I heard God questioning me loud and clear: "When will you go to Canada?" He had me on that one! I quickly changed my response to, "Whenever God says it is time, we will go!" A short time later our married daughter, Rachel, and son-in-law, Jesse moved into our home to start a family and a business, and we drove north to Canada with our van filled with a few of our earthly possessions.

Soon after arriving in the Lower Mainland of British Columbia, we were driving down a country road near Aldergrove. Suddenly we were pulled over by a Royal Canadian Mounted Police officer with siren screaming and lights flashing. To our surprise, he eventually informed us that we were driving through an area known for growing a very potent variety of marijuana (BC Bud), and having California plates on our vehicle made us a bit suspect. He believed that we were who we had said, and did not ask to look in any of the boxes we were transporting. We laughed later when we opened the box closest to the sliding door. It was filled with Ziploc bags of dried spices: oregano, bay leaf, rosemary, mint and basil. Imagine the look on the officer's face if he had opened that box! We had been officially welcomed to Canada.

We lived for a short time in an old school house that had been a church, but was now unused. It was located in the foothills several miles outside of the city of Mission. One night at about two in the morning we were awakened to the noise of people climbing up the wall outside of the room we were using as a bedroom. We were startled, frightened and generally shocked by what was happening. I called the RCMP (feeling a connection from our welcoming event), who said that it would be close to an hour before they could get a car out there. I turned on all of the outside flood lights, kept the inside totally dark, and tried to keep the dispatcher appraised of the progress of the burglars, who were trying to break in through the roof. I had a few tools with me and told Ellie that if they came through a window, I would grab my four foot level and would try to "level" them. My nervous humor did not give her the assurance she needed. Did God bring us all the way to Canada to kill us? Was I going to end up in jail for beating a poor burglar with my vicious level? Then, as suddenly as they had appeared, they disappeared into the night. The officers eventually came with dogs and spotlights, but it was too late. I don't remember sleeping much that night! The next day we were invited to move in with Tim and Laurene Peterson, the President of Foursquare Canada, and his wife. We happily received their hospitality until we were able to find a small townhouse in Abbotsford.

For the next seven years we served the Canadian church in ways that we have been equipped to serve. As a member of the National Team, overseeing the development of "Home-Based" churches, I constantly struggled to understand a concept of ministry that was foreign to me. I had always led with passion and purpose birthed in vision. I was now being asked to "be available" to respond as a resource for local church pastors who would call me with their vision for planting home-based churches. In a church culture where many of the pastors are bi-vocational, the thought of extending oneself beyond trying to maintain one location was not a popular idea. My phone did not ring very often.

At our annual leadership team meetings, I would try each year to find new ways of verbalizing the foundational question of the source of vision-casting. There is such diversity in leadership styles, intensity of personalities, and philosophies of ministry. I was trying to function within a system that placed supreme value on the democratic process of arriving at decisions, and the ultimate inclusion of everyone.

The process of making the decision seemed to be a greater priority than "doing" the actions of the decision. I was often deeply frustrated and disappointed by the process. My personal approach to leadership was to make a decision as quickly and efficiently as possible, and then get on with the work. I finally had to face the fact that my *puzzle piece* did not fit the picture on *their* box.

I have devoted much time to preparing and teaching the *Concepts of the Church* class at our Bible College. I love this class! I love to watch light come into the eyes of students as they think of new ways of being the church. After several years of part-time teaching I felt that I was prepared for a full-time staff position. The school had undergone a major physical expansion program with the addition of a beautiful and functional learning center with a student lounge area and café. The Board of Governors seemed to agree that expanding staff should parallel building expansion, but there was a financial shortage, and there would not be a place for me.

Someone has said that the only thing that is certain is change. Change is an integral part of life and nature. I have always loved the change of seasons that is so apparent in the north: the smells of spring, the warmth of summer, the color of autumn and the quiet rest of winter. This creation picture of changing seasons mirrors our life's journey. Parker Palmer writes,

> There is as much guidance in way that closes behind us as there is in way that opens ahead of us. The opening may reveal our potentials while the closing may reveal our limits – two sides of the same coin, the coin called identity.
>
> As often happens on the spiritual journey, we have arrived at the heart of a paradox: each time a door closes, the rest of the world opens up. All we

need to do is stop pounding on the door that just closed, turn around – which puts the door behind us – and welcome the largeness of life that now lies open to our souls. The door that closed kept us from entering a room, but what now lies before us is the rest of reality. (2000, **Let Your Life Speak***, Parker J. Palmer, Jossey-Bass, A Wiley Co., San Francisco, CA 94103))*

Teaching is at the heart of who I am. Place me in any situation and I will eventually find a way to teach there. This is something I can't not do. I need to be an independent thinker, to have freedom outside of a prescribed job to be creative and original. There are several things that I could do, but are they what I should do?

As I am writing this paragraph, Ellie and I are living in a small apartment in Shoreline, Washington (just north of Seattle). We are calling this a sabbatical time: a time to write, to pray, to think, to reassess our lives, to find our place, to discover God in new places and people, a time to heal from disappointments, a time to *stop pounding on closed doors and welcome the largeness of life that now lies open to our souls.*

Did we completely miss it with our return to Canada? The Apostle Paul gives us a word picture of looking through a glass dimly (one smoked by candle wax), but I have wondered if my looking glass was just totally blackened with no light getting through. But then, there are all of the relationships that have blessed and graced our lives. There are the folks who were in some way encouraged because our paths crossed. There are the many students who have entered ministry with a love for the church and a hope in their hearts that it can be better than it has been. There are fellow pastors who know that we care about their lives and families more than their monthly statistics. There are emerging leaders who have watched us closely, listened to us intently, and have loved us unconditionally. Perhaps these are the things that "called" us back to Canada for a season. As Pastor Barry might say, "This is the main event!"

PART THREE: Is This The Destination?

*"With this I conclude" may be a good ending
to a speech or sermon...
but is an unwise presumption
for an unfinished life!*
DH

*We live in a moment of history
where change is so speeded up
that we begin to see the present
only when it is already disappearing.*
R. D. Laing

*Life must be understood backwards;
but it must be lived forward.*
Soren Kierkegaard

*The years teach much
which the days never knew.*
Ralph Waldo Emerson

SIXTEEN:

Cowboys and Indians

He restores my soul;
He guides me in the paths of righteousness.
Psalm 23:3 NASB

It seems to me that throughout our lives
we walk on two tracks:
the one being how we imagine our lives to be,
the other being the stark reality of what is.
DH

Paris was a perfect town to grow up in as a little boy. It was nestled in rolling hills between the Grand and Nith Rivers. I often spent whole days alone in the woods on the other side of the river from where I lived. It was there that I honed my skills as a trapper and fur trader, a gunslinger and beloved sheriff, a mountain man living as a hermit being pursued by relentless town folk, and a pioneer blazing a trail through the uncharted wilderness. I fished in the river, cooked and ate my catch, living as the king of my secret domain. The bark of White Birch trees provided the

In Search of the Church

parchment I needed to leave a trail of notes and warnings to anyone who might be pursuing me.

I would often meet up with other neighborhood boys as we roamed around Station Hill, a place adorned with a railroad station right out of the old westerns on TV. The railroad tracks, the old steam-belching locomotives, the grumpy station attendant who chased us away from his territory, all were props in our hometown adventure. I loved to play the part of the brave savage, outnumbered by the *pale-faced* gunslingers. I was trained in the ways of the woods from many *moons* of lonely wanderings. With plenty of pigeon feathers around the old Baptist Church, added to Willow branches, dad's finishing nails, and mom's thread, I produced some pretty lethal arrows.

One day, my boyhood sense of justice was threatened by an old Police Sergeant named Jack Bean, who just happened to be in the neighborhood when I was shooting arrows into the sky. He lectured all of us boys about the danger of losing our eyes, and then to my utter shock, he broke my arrows over his knee and walked away carrying the spoils of war. I wonder how he would have responded to the times when all of the cousins would get together out in an open field, and the older boys would shoot *real store-bought* arrows into the sky so high we lost sight of them? All of us would just stand there looking upward with the curiosity that ignorance alone can produce. What goes up must come down! Miraculously, none of us ever ended up with an arrow sticking out of the top of our head.

To cool off in the heat of the day, we would hike over to the wading pool at Lion's Park. It was transformed into a jungle adventure. I remember spending hours diving for "hair" snakes. At the end of the day I would proudly carry home my Coke bottle filled with this dangerous species. My older brother laughingly identified my catch as mere "hairs", not snakes at all. I would shake the jar and excitedly point out the movement of the creatures. To this day, I am certain that I protected children from many potential attacks by not allowing baby snakes to grow up to their full potential.

I loved to walk the iron rails, trying to balance myself without falling into the pit of vipers or the alligator infested waters below. Sometimes, I felt a growing vibration beneath my feet and heard the distant rumbling of an approaching train. This was perhaps the shipment of gold bars we had heard rumors about at the old saloon. At least it was an opportunity to put a penny on the track so that the mighty iron horse could flatten it and make it into something worth so much more.

It seems to me that throughout our lives we walk on two tracks: one being how we imagine our lives to be, the other being the stark reality of what actually is. Like the tracks on Station Hill these two run parallel. One represents our soul, our inner being, our sense of destiny and purpose. There are times in our lives when we feel on track with why we are here. We walk out our destiny in our day-to-day lives with a deep awareness of our value and our contribution. But, that dissipates and we find ourselves again in the physical realm of responsibility, the place where what should be done overshadows what could be done. My experience has been that the two tracks do not often fully overlap each other: the point at which my soul's destiny and my daily routine are the same. How then can I deal with the pain and frustration of this reality? My friend, Rob, once shared this idea with me. He said that we have an inner soul (who we really are, our destiny) and an outer soul (what we do, how we are viewed by others). Our problem comes when we identify ourselves as the outer soul person rather than the inner soul person. This means that we must often revisit the inner soul person to regain a true perspective of destiny and purpose. How many of us identify who we are by what we do, or by the verbal pictures painted by others about us, when in reality there is a deep, passionate inner soul pulsating within?

I worked for a few months in the electrical department at Home Depot. The manager recognized my skills and wanted me to enter a management track so that I could eventually lead one of the new stores opening in Canada. I had the skills to do the job, but from within I heard the voice of destiny saying, "You were created for something else!" I told the manager that I was working there to pay the bills so that I could do what I really wanted to do in ministry. He didn't understand, but I did.

There are readers who feel trapped in the physical realities of jobs and responsibilities to wives and husbands and children and bills. Much of what we understand about our reality is contained in the simple illustration of the two tracks. We do live in a physical universe with all of its shortcomings and restrictions. But, within our souls, we can venture beyond the ordinary into an imagined world where we play a part in God's story. There will always be a conflict. There will always be responsibilities and relationships that demand our time and attention, our life. Revisit your inner soul! Take time to remember that life is precious, that your life is special, that there is still time to be.

SEVENTEEN:

Farmers and Funerals

Faith without works is useless.
James 2:20 NASB

*What would a living faith look like?
How can I make my personal faith come alive?*
DH

Our Japanese neighbors in rural Dinuba, California grew some of the choicest peaches and nectarines in the area. They were kind, gentle and caring people who quietly went about their work and their faith. I was shocked to hear what had been done to them by a godly nation.

After the bombing of Pearl Harbor, December 7, 1941, war hysteria seized the minds and hearts of many Americans. Over the next several months President Roosevelt was pressured to take action against anyone of Japanese descent living in the United States. A resolution was passed, and in February of 1942, 120,000 Japanese were taken from their homes and placed in internment camps across the country. Two thirds of them were American citizens, one-half children. Families were often separated. None of those interned

In Search of the Church

had ever shown any disloyalty to the nation. They were often given less than 48 hours to prepare the few possessions they could carry with them before being evacuated. Many fell prey to unscrupulous fortune hunters who offered them much less than market value for their homes, farms and possessions. These innocent people of Japanese descent were held until 1945. What was the justification for this? They might become spies for the Japanese Emperor. The truth is that only ten people were convicted of spying for Japan during the entire war, all Caucasians!

The local Japanese Methodist pastor had been a young man in the camps. He recalled stories of Bible studies and worship times in the midst of their terror. It always amazes me how true faith flourishes in the darkest times and places. My personal faith was deeply encouraged by one of the stories that I heard from this dark time.

When the evacuation was taking place, some Mennonite farmers approached their Japanese farmer neighbors. They assured them that they would keep watch over their farms while they were gone. Their beautiful expression of faith unfolded like this. The Mennonite community faithfully farmed the Japanese farms until their release in 1945. They cared for the land as if it was their own, cultivating, planting, irrigating and harvesting. They banked the profits in interest bearing accounts. When the Japanese farmers returned, they not only had their farms and homes intact, but were given the money that was raised from the crops that they never had the chance to plant. You want a picture of faith and works… there it is!

One of my many *mini-careers* was working in a funeral home. I did not enjoy most of the work, but there were many opportunities to connect with people at a time of great stress in their lives. In addition to the obvious pain of loss, the families also faced the high cost of the whole funeral process. One day, a funeral was held at the local Japanese church. I noticed that a long table had been set up outside the church, and that there were several people sitting there. As mourners arrived they would all go over to the table and hand an envelope to one of the people seated. A man on a tractor pulling a manure spreader stopped by and quietly delivered his envelope before heading down the road. Later in the afternoon the family came into the funeral home and counted out neat stacks of tens and twenties and fifties. The entire bill was paid in cash, from the envelopes from the Japanese community of faith. I was astounded! I had never seen anything like this, and this was a *Buddhist* Church. I had never seen a Caucasian Christian church respond with this same kind of love and care. Works and faith and works and...

I had developed a friendship with the husband of a lady who attended our church. He had dropped out of church several years before, frustrated with the gulf between spoken faith and lived faith among many of the men of the church. He owned properties in several areas, and invited me to remodel his cabin on the Pacific Ocean. This was a great getaway for Ellie and the girls, as they hung out at the beach while I worked on the cabin. He also had a great little cabin high in the Sierra Nevada Mountains which we used frequently for short breaks from the severe summer heat of the San Joaquin Valley. When they bought a small farm on the valley floor, I was invited to build an office and other creative projects including a large cage for flying squirrels and pheasants.

Harold was a rough and tough mountain man, a multi-generational logger who loved to work the high country. He operated a sawmill and hardware store in the foothills, and was known throughout the region as a just man who would help anyone in need. We had numerous conversations about life and church and faith. One day he announced to me that he was an atheist. I laughed out loud and told him that he was too smart to be an atheist. He smiled broadly and agreed wholeheartedly. I think it was a little test he had prepared for me: the local pastor, the church boy!

When the time came for Ellie and me to build our first home, Harold let me know that anything he could help me with by way of materials would be sold to me at his cost. I made many trips up the mountain with my little Chevy LUV pickup, many times so overloaded that it barely waddled down the hill. To my amazement, once a month a donation designated for "The Hageys" for the exact amount of materials I had purchased would appear in the offering. My *non-church-attending* brother was modeling a kind of faith-works practice that challenged me to the core.

I shared this story earlier, but it bears repeating here. When Steve became pastor at Wellspring, he and the leadership team made a decision to apply works to faith. For each month of that summer, one Sunday was designated as a "Work Sunday". A list was gathered of projects needing to be done for seniors and shut-ins and single moms and folks too sick to work. We all gathered on those Sundays in work clothes, carrying shovels and rakes and hammers and saws. We worshipped briefly together, and then divided into teams with specific assignments. The children and youth were delighted to be able to be with family; to be doing something for someone in need, and I'm sure to miss another "sit-still" sermon. The recipients of this care were overwhelmed, many responding through tears saying that they had never experienced kindness like this before.

What would a living faith look like? James says that a "dead" faith has no works accompanying it. How can I make my personal faith come alive? If we are so concerned that we might slip in to some "social gospel" mode, that we refuse to be involved in the practical care of fellow humans, what is our faith really all about?

EIGHTEEN:

Gender Gap

*There is neither male nor female;
for you are all one in Christ Jesus.*
Galatians 3:28 NASB

*We have deprived the church
of half of its giftedness
by denying women
full participation in its life.*
DH

Mom was really the spiritual leader in our home. I would plead with her to let me stay home Sunday night with my dad to watch the "Wonderful World of Disney" on our little oval-shaped black and white TV. Being in the church building was important to her, but her faith extended far beyond its walls. I have mentioned in other chapters about her kindness in caring for the elderly lady next door. Whenever a need was brought to her attention, she would respond quickly and quietly with practical and emotional support. She taught us that God loved us and that we could accomplish good things with our lives.

Opel Reddin impacted my life more than any other teacher or professor. She taught for years at Central Bible College in Springfield, Missouri. Her contribution to my life and scores of other students was this: she stimulated us to use our minds and hearts to creatively serve God in ways that matched our uniqueness. She freed us to "color outside the lines" in our lives and ministries. I treasure the brief moments spent in her classroom and the personal conversations about life that impacted my view of myself and my understanding of destiny. She completed her earthly assignment on November 19, 2006.

Sister Aimee (Aimee Semple McPherson) grew up in a little farming community in Southern Ontario. I visited the little museum at the general store and post office in Salberg and was amazed at the documents that covered the walls. They included posters of meetings and newspaper clippings and stories of healings and feeding the hungry during the Great Depression, world-wide revival and new churches and the birth of the International Church of the Foursquare Gospel. A small group of elderly ladies sat in a knitting circle outside the museum. They pointed me to the place of her birth just up the road. I stood looking at the plaque that was the historical marker for this amazing woman's birthplace, reading of her exploits for the Kingdom of God and the impact of a young farm-girl from the village.

Ellie has been my life's partner for thirty-eight years. There is no possible way that I could have done the things I have done without her. One of my great joys in life has been to help her discover her gifts and destiny, her passions and dreams. She is filled with compassion for the weak and downtrodden. Her mercy is expressed in finding practical ways to alleviate pain and suffering. By the time this book is published, she will have taken a second team to Africa to minister hands-on care to dozens of AIDS orphans in

Zimbabwe and Malawi. She has raised both awareness and finances for projects providing "fistula" surgery for outcast women. When a mudslide in Nicaragua buried most of a mountain village, Ellie joined a team that ministered there. She has mentored many young women, each trying to find their place in life and ministry.

She wrote a brief article that was published online in Globalgirl Network, One-By-One and on a United Nations' website about one of her fundraising experiences:

Fighting Fistulas, One by One
By Ellie Hagey

A few weeks ago I attended a film fest with my oldest daughter, Tonya Sargent. One of the films we watched was a documentary called "Love, Labor, Loss" that told the story of women with fistulas, or holes, caused by obstructed labor. Most of the time the baby dies and because of prolonged pressure on the mother's soft tissue often a hole is formed, allowing urine to leak continuously.

Fistulas mainly affect women who live in poverty in the developing world and can't obtain quality health care, mostly in Africa, Asia and some Arab states. As a result of this condition, they are often shunned and ostracized by society. According to the United Nations Population Fund (UNFPA), obstetric fistula affects an estimated 50,000 to 100,000 women around the world every year. After watching the film, we were introduced to two women in Seattle who had learned that $300 would pay for fistula surgery for one woman. They started a group called "One by One" and the idea is to create a giving circle of ten women. The leader hosts a circle, donates $30 and asks the other nine participants to do the same.

I was so inspired by these women from Seattle. Sometimes the need seems so big you wonder, "How could I, one person, possibly make a difference?" I realized by very little effort I could significantly change the life of one woman.

With the help of some friends we planned a Saturday brunch. I sent out invitations and talked about what I had learned to whoever would listen. I wondered: "Would women catch the vision of this and want to help? Would we be able to raise the $300?"

I needn't have worried. The day of the brunch, women began arriving at my home and they placed their donation in a little basket I had brought back from Africa. We enjoyed breakfast together in my garden, then went inside to view the documentary and share our response on what we had seen. Many were moved to tears seeing how our "sisters around the globe" had suffered giving birth. I read the poem "Still I Rise" by Maya Angelou to honor the courage of these women who suffer so much but still go on. A friend brought bleeding heart seedlings for each woman. We were told it would bloom next year, symbolizing hope and new life for the women who will benefit from our day together.

We ended our time by joining our hands in a circle and speaking out our hopes and prayers for our sisters across the seas. When the money was counted we had raised $1200, enough for four women to have the necessary surgery and also have their lives transformed. Some of the women in the group expressed interest in hosting their own circle.

I envision our giving circle as a pebble thrown into the water. First one circle forms, then another and another. My heart was warmed to know that other women, here in Canada, could catch the vision of how we are all connected. The privilege of living in this country also brings with it the responsibility to help those who are less fortunate than us.

This week I was in Seattle taking training to become a Doula. At our lunch break I mentioned the brunch we had and also about "One by One." Afterwards one of the women at our table came and asked for my email because she too wanted to host a giving circle. I was thrilled.
And so the circle widens.

Our daughters, Tonya, Rachel and Sarah have taught me so much about the incredible contribution that women are making in our world. Each of them has found ways to creatively express their care for the poor and the outcast. Each has made a trip to Africa to care for AIDS orphans and abused women. Each has been involved in raising funds and awareness for marginalized peoples. Each is a wonderful gift to me and to the world. May I never say or do anything that places limits on their God-given destinies.

Several young ladies have been a part of our Emerge Community house/café church in the last couple of years. Some of them are graduates of a local Bible College which they attended as part of a process to fulfill a sense of God's calling on their lives to be involved in meaningful ministry. Nearing graduation, one of them was informed by a teacher/pastor that she really had two strokes against her for future ministry involvement: she was single and she was female! The prejudicial judgment levied against her was disheartening for her to say the least. Regardless of her gifts, passion, abilities and experience, she could be deemed second-class as far as church ministry is considered because of her gender and marital status.

This is the tragic message that most women have heard overtly or subtly from male-dominated leadership for years. It is not the message of Jesus! He identified the true beauty and value of all, prepared a place at the table for everyone, regardless of race, ethnicity, gender or social status. Men... we have been wrong in our assumptions about rulership and headship and submission for far too long. We have deprived the church of half of its giftedness by denying women full participation in its life.

Another of our young ladies worked as receptionist, secretary, purchasing agent, day-care facilitator, bulletin-maker, and leaky-roof fixer for a local church. The newly hired senior pastor called her a "fat cow" and a "bitch" to her face, the whole time excusing any discomfort she might have felt on the basis of his British upbringing. He verbally and emotionally abused every female staff member in some way or another. The all-male church board was fully supportive of his introductory sermons on "submitting" to him as pastor, and women "submitting" to their husbands. The demeaning tone and content of his put-women-in-their-place message could not in any way be considered in alignment with the good news of Jesus' gospel. She finally left that very demeaning and painful situation with our full support and blessing. He is fortunate to not be facing legal charges.

I am thrilled and blessed that Jen was chosen to become the senior pastor of one of Canada's Foursquare churches located in Powell River, British Columbia. We had spent time together at Emerge, and we knew her heart and passion to lead a group of people to maturity in Christ. After considering male leaders for this position, the Foursquare leadership appointed Jen. She became the youngest (at 25) female senior pastor in Canada, and she is single. We stay connected and excitedly watch her leading an older church into a time of refocusing and change.

It has not been my purpose to present a theological argument for the idea of women in ministry but rather to tell the story of my journey and my own discoveries on this important subject. There are excellent books that approach this subject with respect and Biblical scholarship. One of the most thorough and meaningful books is **Why Not Women** (2000, Loren Cunningham and David J. Hamilton, YWAM Publishing, Seattle, WA 98155). I could not even begin to present a reasonable discussion of women in ministry in this short chapter, but strongly encourage you to get this book and prayerfully study its message.

Cunningham writes:

I see every little girl growing up knowing she is valued, knowing she is made in the image of God, and knowing that she can fulfill all the potential He has put within her. I see the Body of Christ recognizing leaders whom the Holy Spirit indicates, the ones whom He has gifted, anointed, and empowered without regard to race, color, or gender. This generation will be one that simply asks, "Who is it that God wants?" There will be total equality of opportunity, total equality of value, and a quickness to listen to and follow the ones the Holy Spirit sets apart.

Hamilton concludes:

It is time for us to rethink some of our oldest beliefs and traditions. It is time for us to repent for whatever ways we have hindered God's work and misread His Word. It is time for us to release women to be all that God has called them to be.

My heart-felt response is, May it be so!

NINETEEN:

What Did Jesus Say?

Jesus said to him, "Follow Me."
John 1:43 NASB

*The point is:
Is this what Jesus has in mind
for His church?*
DH

Pastors understand the ongoing pressure to succeed in ministry. Whether it comes from within, or from our peers, or from church boards and growth committees, it is real. It can be as subtle as a question from a fellow pastor about how things are going at our church, or as overt as a monthly report required by the Head Office that asks for numerical evidence of conversions and attendance at our meetings as well as confirmation of increasing income. This is such a personal thing for many in the ministry. We want to be perceived as successful, and seem willing to try almost anything to get our numbers up. Huge industries have arisen to respond to this felt need.

Try an internet search on the subject of "Church Growth Principles". There are well over a million entries on this subject alone, not including other suffixes such as: institutes, movement, statistics, international, software, ideas, strategies, barriers and magazines. A quick review of a few of these tells me that they have vastly different approaches, some in total disagreement with others. Here are just a few illustrations: *The Church Is Not A Business / How To Operate Your Church On Business Principles; Evangelism Made Easy / Church Growth When The Formulas Don't Work; The Pastor's Personal Pocket Guide To Church Growth Ratios / Common Sense Church Growth.* Of course I realize that the underlying conviction behind most of these is that we are called to reach people for Jesus. The point is: Is this what Jesus has in mind for His church?

Another enticing method of producing the "numbers" is to copy what a successful church has done. I have attended an embarrassingly large number of these events. A church somewhere begins to experience rapid numerical growth, and then they produce a seminar to transfer their success to me. Sounds good, let's do it! The problem with this method is fairly obvious to me in retrospect. Someone once said, "Doug…You are unique just like everybody else in the whole world." I am not the pastor of that successful church. I do not have her or his gifts, passion, abilities, experience or personality. I cannot copy who they are, (although I have seen many little "clones" of certain visible leaders). I have not walked their journey and do not know the pain of their pathway. I do not know the process which God has walked them through to bring them to this point in their distinct timeline of ministry. My church is not located in their community or culture. I do not know about the unseen forces that have been brought to bear on them because of the prayers of intercessors over the years. I do not know God's special plan for them in His overall scheme for Kingdom growth. Yet, I am in attendance at a seminar to try, in a few hours, to glean ideas that might help my church grow. Yes, there are some transferable principles that can be applied universally, but it is foolishness to think that I can move God's hand to do the same thing in my context, simply by copying their methods. The numerous seminar notebooks standing in neat rows on my bookcase just responded with a rousing "amen!"

A couple of years ago as I was preparing for our first meeting with a group of college students in our home, I distinctly heard an inner voice speaking to me: "Read the 'red text'... What did Jesus say?" This captivated my thinking. I had taught for years from Paul's writings to the churches, had used the gospel stories as springboards for topical sermons on manifold subjects. The Book of Revelation had occasionally provided the intro to my thoughts about world conditions and possible future headlines. The Old Testament had been referred to often as a signpost for the *really important* part of the Bible found in the New Testament. But, I had never spent much time on the actual words of Jesus, had never heard much preaching from the "red" text. I started to ask myself a series of questions. If I am truly a follower of Jesus, should I know what my leader taught? It seems that I had focused on everybody else's commentary on what He had said. Is it possible that the essence of the gospel is contained in His words? Should I call myself a "Christian" or would it be more accurate to be called a "Paulian" or "Johnian" or "Davidian"? Of course I jest, but the point is that we need to revisit the words that our Master spoke to be able to accurately interpret and apply the rest of the black text.

At the risk of being considered simplistic, I want to review three ideas from Jesus' own words to us. If they are true, they should stand the test of time, being relevant to all generations. They should also stand the tests of geography and culture, being applicable to all peoples in all places. I say this from a conviction that truth is universal and should not be viewed or applied through a North American Christian grid. I recall the times when I was preparing to speak in other continents, and needed to ask myself if my message was truly Biblical, truly the heart of Christ, or if it was tainted by my own culture's perceived social and economic advantages. This was an important question to ask when I was about to address a group of Indian pastors who lived in poverty, leading small house-churches in the rubber plantations of Kerala State in South-Western India. I was forced by their reality to present truth that was faithful to historically biblical foundations.

Jesus spoke many amazing things while walking on the earth. He constantly brought people back to issues of the heart. He presented a simplified faith in the midst of a Jewish culture that had a complicated system of laws and rules that alienated people from their God and from each other. I will discuss three of His sayings.

A Pharisee lawyer asked Jesus a difficult question in Matthew 22. What is the most important commandment in the Law? *The Great Commandment*, Jesus said, was to love God with all your heart, soul and mind and love your neighbor as yourself. How much simpler could it be? *Love God – Love People*! I remember the day when I asked a young female check-out clerk how she was doing. She responded that I likely really didn't want to know. When I assured her of my interest, she tearfully told me of her very sick child who she had to leave at home so she could work as his provider. She really wanted to be with him and the pain of her situation was imprinted on her young face. When I asked for his name and if it would be alright for Ellie and I to pray for him, she was overwhelmed with gratitude. We paid for our groceries and prayed for him and her when we got to the car. I don't remember seeing her again, but I believe that we participated with God in something He was already doing in her heart.

In Search of the Church

On Mothers' Day a few of our house-church youth joined us as we took long-stemmed roses down to the Main and Hastings area of inner-city Vancouver. Mothers, whose painful history of abuse was etched deeply into their faces, reached out to us in grateful surprise to receive one simple acknowledgement of their motherhood. The joy of being humanized again brought tears and shouts and laughter.

Our neighbor, Lori Jo, was forced to move from her condemned house into the house on the other side of us. The new location was so rat-infested, that one afternoon I came across a frenzied circle of some 40 rats, each staking its claim to a portion of a leftover McDonald's hamburger that had been tossed into the yard. I fed them rat poison for days, until dozens of their corpses began to show up inside and outside of the buildings. Ellie spent many hours loading dumpsters with garbage. The Emerge kids helped repair holes in the ceilings, installed new drywall, painted, installed doors and carpet. At one of our Emerge gatherings, Lori-Jo sat in our living room and shared her heart-wrenching story of addiction and abuse, and how she was on a pathway to being clean. She was grateful for every little thing that we did to make her life a bit better. She continues in her own pilgrimage of personal faith.

I grew up with a very rigid idea of evangelism. True evangelism always ended with the "deal" being closed with the "sinner's prayer." Success was contingent upon a numerical accounting of "new converts" and failure was as easily defined by negative numbers.

My friend, Jim Henderson of "Off The Map", recently wrote a very insightful article about the Four Approaches To Evangelism. He takes a look at historical methods that have become the standard for evangelicals.

Man Evangelism, like Billy Graham, is centered in the Man as the Evangelist. What began as city-wide crusades has evolved into international TV and satellite events. Many have copied Billy's method as they speak to masses of people, give an invitation to respond to Christ, and then move on to the next event.

Message Evangelism began sometime after WW II when people wanted to have some active involvement in the evangelism process. They wrote tracts that told about the "lostness" of men and their need for Christ. I remember handing out "The Four Spiritual Laws" to many strangers on the street. This method does not require me to speak with or even get involved in someone's life in any way. The message is concise in its explanation of what a person needs to know and do to become a Christian. Anyone can stick a tract on a parked car or leave it in a motel room or on the table at a restaurant (with or without a tip for the server). I recently received an envelope in the mail with no return address. Inside there were three tracts with no personal note or contact information. I could read about Born Again or Jesus is Coming or Free Beautiful Homes Given Away in the Perfect City. I have no idea who sent them or if they even know who I am.

Movement Evangelism allows people to show kindness or special care to others without having to preach at them in the process. Caring for the poor, offering pregnancy counseling, teaching English as a second language (ESL) to new immigrants, providing after-school childcare for children of single parents and so on, gives opportunity for Christians to be connected with not-yet-Christians in meaningful ways.

Moment Evangelism is less of an event and more of a spiritual practice of integrating our faith into every aspect of our daily lives and the natural connections with people that we encounter every day. If we believe that God is at work in everyone's life, then we can accept our brief interactions with people as participation in a partnership with God. He has already begun the process of loving people, we simply join Him in what He is already doing. I do not have to find ways to initiate the process or somehow feel responsible to conclude the process of God's involvement in their lives.

My response to The Great Commandment has more to do with being real in my approach to God and others than it has to do with following certain prescribed religious exercises. As far as loving God goes, my definition of *authentic worship* is : A lifestyle of connecting with God wherever I am, as a "real" person. So what about loving people? What does it mean to be authentic in relationships? I believe it is a lifestyle of connecting with people as a real human being, recognizing and appreciating their incredible value as God's creation.

How can I know if I am loving God? I ask myself questions like these: Am I continuing to be spiritually hungry for more of God? Do I admit spiritual dryness when it occurs in me? Am I able to convey to God what is "really" going on in my heart and mind on a regular basis?

Am I loving people? Do I give any of my time to those who serve me? Do I care about what is going on in the lives of others? Do I have a close friend? How do I deal with loneliness? Is my connection with people at church more like a living organism or a business arrangement? Am I honest about myself: my gifts, abilities, shortcomings, doubts and fears? Am I mentoring someone to help them reach their potential?

What last words did Jesus have for his followers? **The Great Purpose or Destiny** is found in Matthew 28 when Jesus said: "Go and make disciples of all the nations!" When we look at the programs and expenditures of our church, how much of our time, talent, money and energy is being invested in making disciples? Do we have a clear process that we are following that will result in mature followers of Jesus? If we took the time to evaluate every program and event that we present, in light of the "making disciples" question, what would we continue doing, and what would we need to stop doing? Are there entry points through which pre-Christians can easily connect with members of the church? Are these points relevant to the needs of the people within the circle of our church's influence? Could we offer ESL classes to new immigrants to help them into our culture? Are there single parents who need affordable childcare? Are there children who need after-school activities to keep them from the dangers of street life? Are young professionals in need of a safe place to drink coffee and pursue spirituality without judgment? Are college students looking for a place that feels like "home" just to hang out together?

Once people have connected with us, are we providing a kind and authentic faith that attracts them to the Jesus that we follow? Once they are attracted, are we providing opportunities to "reason together" around scripture in a way that responds honestly to their questions? Do we have a plan to help them discern their unique gifts and ministries? Is there an intentional pathway to support the process of developing new leaders? Are there opportunities for ministry involvement inside and outside of the church? We simply must view what we do in terms of the final words of Jesus.

When Jesus was emotionally moved by lost people He gave us **The Great Method** of evangelism. In Matthew 9 He said that we should ask Him for workers. A few years ago I heard a tape series and read a manual by Robert Logan and Neil Cole titled: **Raising Leaders for the Harvest** (1992-1995, ChurchSmart Resources, Alta Loma, CA 91701). They introduced the idea of raising people for the harvest from the harvest, by seeing potential Christian leadership in people who have not committed their lives to Jesus. This requires looking with the eyes of Jesus at who He is raising up to work with us in His Kingdom work.

In addition to this pre-viewing of leaders, we must also be committed to nurturing relationships with those who are raw material in the school of leadership development, and be especially discerning to identify those who are emerging leaders.

I need the compassion of Christ to see the multitudes as "leaderless" sheep and respond by "beseeching the Lord of the harvest to send out workers into *His* harvest".

Would you join me in returning to the "red text"?

TWENTY:

Prototype

*New wine must be put into
fresh wineskins.*
Luke 5:38 NASB

*I had struggled for so long
trying to understand the true essence of church.
Was there a simple definition of church?*
DH

Fresh air, great food and lots of rest, the rugged mountains, and the enormous Sugar Pines and Redwoods all collaborated to create a time and space to listen for God's voice. I was reading a book by Michael E. Gerber titled: ***The E-Myth***, (out of print) about the new way of doing business that was birthed in America that has led to a world-wide explosion of franchises. The old paradigm of Mom and Pop stores operated by hands-on owners who were the resident experts had given way to a new breed of stores. These businesses could be duplicated endlessly due to the simplification of all of their procedures into written manuals. A person of average intelligence and education could be trained to operate the systems. The need for a large number of experts had been removed. I found this to be fascinating reading.

Part way through the week at the little mountain cabin, the *"penny dropped"* for me. For those not familiar with that expression, my version of it goes like this: as a child I frequented the gumball machine on the main street of our little town. In those days you got a handful of gum for a penny. You placed your coin in a little groove and turned the handle. When you heard the penny hit the bottom of the metal container, you knew that gum was on the way. So, it was a light bulb moment, the bell rang, the dust settled, I saw the light!

Gerber zoomed in on the key idea of this new business model. The "franchise prototype" was the entity that the new business owners focused their time and energy upon. They worked on their business instead of just in their business. By understanding the exact procedures involved in doing any of the functions within their business, and writing a simple and clear description of those procedures, they created a way of duplicating in other locations exactly what they were doing in their current location. We are so accustomed to shopping at Office Depot, Home Depot, Best Buy, McDonalds, Burger King and many other franchises that we unconsciously expect that their store in Seattle will be exactly like the one in Vancouver. Why is that true? They all operate under a prototype model which they developed at a first location that is being duplicated in precise detail in each new location. These businesses operate training courses for new employees that facilitate the immediate insertion of the employees into the day-to-day functions of the business. I experienced this process firsthand when I was employed for a few months at a Home Depot store in California. A number of new recruits were oriented at the same time. We were quickly walked through a number of manuals dealing with store procedures on issues like returns, competitive price matching, safety, handling incoming stock, dealing with customers and so on. All of us spent a few minutes operating each piece of equipment to receive our certification as operators. It was quite an amazing plan to get us participating in the company.

I had struggled for so long trying to understand the true essence of church. Was there a simple definition of church? Were there basic elements that were always present in a church? Could the list of those elements be applied universally to all churches of all times, cultures and places? This is where the *penny dropped* on that mountainside! Gerber's explanation of the franchise prototype gripped my heart and mind, not as a possible business solution, but as a way of looking at the church and church pioneering. I can feel the discomfort that some of you are experiencing as I seem to be applying business terms to the church. It is not the application of business terminology that inspires me. It is the idea that there may be a prototype of the church that is simple, duplicable, and a plumb line for assessing our progress. What if I took the time to understand all of the details that make up a church, and then develop a prototype that could be duplicated in other places? What if I used that prototype as a guideline to help me make decisions of what to value, what to add or delete, what is worthy of the time, money and talent of the church? I concluded that such a prototype might be possible and that I should commit myself to try to discover it.

Over the past years I have discovered pieces of this prototype. Recalling my journey in the last chapters has helped to uncover some of these pieces. It is not complete, it is still in process, but this chapter moves us beyond the hints imbedded in my stories toward a fuller description of some of the keys from my journey. Here are a few of my discoveries.

Church is mystery.

Ministry is the profession of fools and clowns telling everyone who has ears to hear and eyes to see that life is not a problem to be solved, but a mystery to be entered into. Henri Nouwen

If church is just a business or an institution, then we have a high level of control over its development, progress and design. But it is a living organism in the constant process of being renewed, revitalized and animated. Jesus did say in Matthew 16:18, "I will build My church." Given the way in which He builds it, through breathing new life into people who are dead spiritually, I see this process as more like The Creation in which God breathed animating life into Adam's soul and spirit, rather than a bricks and mortar building, or an accounting of adherents. The church is alive, growing through stages of development and understanding, in the process of being built by Jesus day-by-day.

It is the life of church that is mystery. There is little mystery in the programs or the business of doing church on a weekly basis. So much of what we do can be attributed to our mathematical calculations, our ability to make decisions about how and where we will meet, who will be paid to lead our meetings, and how we will present our information about the Christ who builds churches. Our budgets and business meetings, our flow charts and calendars, our boards and committees, and our bulletins and orders-of-service, are all evidence of our perceived ability to build churches. But in reality, the Builder of churches does it through mystery, not math.

The New Testament word "musterion" literally means "to shut the mouth." It may be described as one of those moments when something so overwhelming happens to us that we simply say "wow!" Scripture talks about the *"mystery of the faith"* (Timothy 3:9), *"God's mystery, which is Christ"* (Colossians 2:2), *"the mystery of the Kingdom of God"* (Mark 4:11), and the *"mystery of the gospel"* (Ephesians 6:19). Only God can change a human heart! Only He can transform a hardened, proud, self-sufficient, self-centered, addicted, arrogant soul, into a tender-hearted, humble, interdependant servant. This is the mystery! It causes me to stand in awe and simply say "wow!"

If building the church is about this mystery, and not about my abilities, then I should be first in line to proclaim that good news has set me free and that *whosoever will* may come to gather with me in my celebration of this unfathomable gift from God. His gift is inclusive, is my church exclusive? His gift is invaluable, have I cheapened it by familiarity? His gift is a mystery, can I explain it?

The Bible is not primarily a *math text* filled with equations and formulas in which everything adds up to neatly defined answers. It is really more like an art book filled with stories and pictures and journeys painted in words. Math is a fixed science with proven formulas that always work. Art contains mystery, attempting to reveal the hidden heart of the artist.

Church is two or more people sharing their lives together around the wonderful mystery of being changed by Christ from the inside out.

Church is universal and local.

As Ellie and I have traveled to several countries, we have been blessed by the wonderful beauty and diversity of the universal church. People everywhere who have been changed by the mystery of the gospel are one family in Christ. Cultural expressions of devotion to Christ are a little bit like the incredible diversity of design in nature, the varieties of plants and animals all pointing to a generous, extravagant and creative God. It is painful to see how the imposed restrictions and limitations of western colonization have disrupted or destroyed the beauty of these local expressions. Why would we expect a village pastor in East Africa to wear a three-piece western business suit instead of his brightly colored loose-fitting robes? Why would we replace the sounds of indigenous instruments with electric guitars and keyboards? Over the years, we have exported the local Christian traditions from our culture, and tried to impose them on the universal church. I am saddened by the loss of so much of the local beauty of the church.

In the Book of Revelation chapter 5, verse 9 (NIV) we read:

You are worthy to take the scroll and to open its seals, because you were slain, and with your blood you purchased men for God from every tribe and language and people and nation.

The whole context of Christ's gift of salvation is the "cosmos": the world's diverse tribes, languages, peoples and nations. The unity of the universal church is centered in its common relationship to Christ ("Everybody who belongs to Jesus, belongs to everybody who belongs to Jesus"); its diversity is centered in its common Creator.

It is true that there are elements in every culture that are evil. The problem that I have witnessed is based upon redefining "syncretism" (the blending of two opposite belief systems into one, like blending pagan practices into Christianity) to mean the blending of culture and Christian faith. This misuse of terms has led to the painful ripping from local believers of unique cultural expressions, and has created forms of legalism that bind people from being authentically themselves.

I do not expect that my expression of worship will be the standard in Heaven. (That is not a big revelation for me to grasp!). I fully expect that a creative blend of expressions from the world's peoples will be heard around the throne of our creative God, not to mention new forms of worship that none of us has experienced before. That sounds like a lot of fun!

Church is love.

Now that you've cleaned up your lives by following the truth, love one another as if your lives depended on it. I Peter 1:22 The Message

Just before we moved to Seattle a few months ago, our neighbor, Lori Jo came over to say goodbye. Her final remark to us was, "Thank-you for your unconditional love for me!" Tears welled up in my eyes as I felt God's heart for her all over again. She still carries baggage from years of being abused and misunderstood by so many, including some church folks. She is continuing on a spiritual pilgrimage, upon which we have shared only a short distance as travelers together. There could have been no greater expression of gratitude for us to hear from her. Through God's grace we had become a safe place for her during some critical days of her journey. Only because we had experienced the mystery of God's unconditional love, could we pass the same onto her.

Too many times I have heard the church described as judgmental, harsh, and uncaring. The unconditional love of God led Him to give the gift of greatest value so that we could reconnect with Him. To be His followers, we too must be unconditional lovers of those created in His image. It might just cost us something too!

Church is a living organism made up of many parts.

The whole body, being fitted and held together by that which every joint supplies, according to the proper working of each individual part, causes the growth of the body for the building up of itself in love. Ephesians 4:16 NASB

It was never intended to be a super-star endeavor, this church that Jesus was raising up. It was to be a team, a body made up of various unique parts that would each fulfill a role that would ultimately result in a healthy, loving, animated church. There are certain more visible roles or gifts given by Christ to the church, but they too exist to "equip the saints for the work of service" (Ephesians 4:12). Unity in the church only functions when we recognize and appreciate the diversity of gifts and ministries that Christ has given. None of us have the full picture of what church can be, none of us alone have all of the abilities to cause it to operate as a healthy, life-giving organism. Recognizing our need for one another, and the beauty of the composite picture created by the collaboration of us all, is at the heart of understanding church as Jesus intended it.

If church is only business or institution, then those who are the executives of the corporation perceive their roles as being of paramount importance, and the roles of all others as subservient to themselves. This is totally opposite to the picture that Christ gave us of servant leaders who lay down their lives (time, place of honor) for others. Everyone has value, everyone has a place at the table, everyone adds to the beauty and function of the whole church.

Christian A. Schwarz in his books, ***Natural Church Development*** (1996, ChurchSmart Resources, Carol Stream, IL 60188) and ***Paradigm Shift in the Church*** (1999, ChurchSmart Resources, Carol Stream, IL 60188)

has captured the idea of church being organic rather than technocratic. After researching one thousand congregations in 32 countries, on six continents, he concludes that healthy, growing churches share certain common DNA. He narrows his findings to eight "quality characteristics" that appear over and over again in these churches. He points out that the adjective that he uses to describe each characteristic is the real key to understanding its full meaning. The eight are:

> *Empowering Leadership*
> *Gift-oriented Ministry*
> *Passionate Spirituality*
> *Functional Structures*
> *Inspiring Worship Services*
> *Holistic Small Groups*
> *Need-oriented Evangelism*
> *Loving Relationships*

Schwarz then describes what he calls the "Minimum Factor". In a business model leaders place their energies and finances upon their perceived areas of greatest strength. In an organic model, those energies are placed upon areas of greatest weakness, so that the whole organism can grow and flourish without being held back by those weaknesses. He uses a picture of a barrel with eight staves (wooden slats making up its sides), each differing in length. When he pours water (God's blessing upon His church) into the barrel, it begins to leak at the point of the shortest stave. The only way to retain the water or increase its volume is to increase the length of the shortest stave, and the next shortest and so on. This view of organic church growth recognizes that "every joint" supplies something of importance to the whole organism; and that weakness results from people not functioning in their unique gifted capacity, or who need encouragement or instruction in how to function. His model and his eight essential qualities for healthy churches may not be all there is to know on this subject, but he has opened the door to a way of thinking about the health of churches that should not be overlooked.

Church is a living organism with wonderful potential, including a real potential for disease, but great potential for healing of itself from within, and unlimited potential for taking over whole geographical areas through healthy growth.

Church is community.

We are a family of people in relationship with Jesus and each other. The word translated in New Testament scripture as "fellowship" is "koinonia", which means partnership, communion, participation and communication. People in our disjointed and dysfunctional society long for some semblance of meaningful family connection. Where can they go for authentically unselfish relationship? If we are living a lifestyle of caring community in which we are growing in our personal faith while walking with our fellow faith travelers, then we can become that connection for them. If church is just a place that we go to do certain religious rituals, it will appear to be an unwelcoming sub-culture for those who seek real relationship.

During the Emergent 2007 Conference, Denise Van Eck shared some insights on the idea of starting community groups. She led a team to facilitate small groups for Mars Hill in Michigan, a church of some ten thousand members. She said that community is intrinsic and must grow and develop a bit like raising kids, each different from the other. We can create the atmosphere but cannot really control community, rather discover it. Her suggestion is that we start with mission rather than models for these groups, and think in terms of neighborhood "parishes" where the kingdom is already present through followers of Jesus. Within each parish there are oppressed and needy people, garbage on the streets, or whatever other need exists in that unique setting. Community then, looks a lot like life, and as groups meet they can hear God's voice together in "community discernment" to gain understanding of their mission. She suggests that as we call people together to discern mission, they will discern identity and grow in community.

There is an ongoing debate about whether a church can be "missional" (described later in this chapter as carrying on God's mission on earth) and still have a strong sense of community. Which is the "cart" and which is the "horse"? Does it have to be one or the other? It seems that in times of change and shift in our thinking, we tend to swing past the center point of balance and over-emphasize what has been lacking. An example of this is the birth of para-church organizations that resulted from a perceived inadequacy of the church to engage in mission. The youth of churches who would have normally sat and listened to sermons about missions, or listened to missionary reports about far away lands, joined Youth With A Mission (YWAM) and Operation Mobilization (OM) and dozens of other organizations to actually do mission's things. From my personal experience, I cannot say that a strong sense of faith community emerged from within these groups. Part of the problem has been their insistence on being "para-church" and therefore not church in nature. My problem with that philosophy is that church is being defined as an organization or institution, rather than people of God moving together in mission and growing together in relationship. Church is church!

Jesus commanded us to "go and make disciples." I cannot imagine that He had "go to a church building" in mind when He said that, but rather that we should go to our neighborhood and beyond in the process of disciple-making. The idea of making disciples requires some kind of devotion to being together over a period of time with a group of people. Sounds a bit like community doesn't it?

In John 21 Jesus asks Peter if he loves Him and then responds with a series of commands for Peter to "keep, graze, pasture, tend and shepherd" the lambs and sheep. This too is a picture of long-term involvement in the lives of people in a relationship that provides care and facilitates growth.

When asked what the greatest commandment was, Jesus responded by saying that we should love God with our whole being and love our neighbor as much as we love ourselves. Community should cause us to grow in our love for God and our love for our "parish", our neighborhood. Community should bring healing to broken people, maturity to learning followers, opportunity for spiritual gifts to be shared with each other, a sense of family togetherness, and discernment of our mission to others.

In August 2000 I did a study to discover what the New Testament had to say about how we should assemble together. I was surprised by the simplicity of what I found. In Hebrews 10 we are told to "not forsake our own assembling together" and even to increase doing so as times get tougher. So, we are directed to meet often. Secondly our meetings should be creative. In 1 Corinthians 14:26, Colossians 3:12-17, and Ephesians 5:15-21 we are presented with a picture of variety, participation and creative involvement of the members of the faith community. Thirdly, we should meet with purpose. In Acts 2:42-47 we read about the life of the early church. They shared teachings and fellowship, broke bread and prayed together, shared all things in common, gathered daily in both temple and homes, praised God and had favor with all the people. It was in this context that "The Lord was adding to their number day by day."

It seems to me that if we are fully devoted to each other in love and fully devoted to God, we will be a missional community touching the lives of our neighbors with genuine love and compassion. There is no question that the church has tended to consume the love and gifts of Christ upon itself, but people truly in love with God will always be truly in love with their neighbor because doing so is part of the nature of the God we say we love and follow. Given the fact that we can move so quickly to focus upon ourselves and our own needs, it will be essential that we continue to "stimulate one another to love and good deeds" (Hebrews 10:24 NASB) so that we don't distract ourselves from doing mission while also doing community.

Church is "salt and light" in the world.

A sub-culture is created by a group that separates itself from the mainstream of its culture through several means. Its people may have a certain way of dressing, use words or phrases that are unique to them and understood only within their group, have certain common ways of thinking about life and the issues of life, read and write literature or books that agree with the way they think and act, may choose to live in close proximity with others in their group, spend most of their spare time together with each other, require certain steps to be taken to become a member of their group, exhibit attitudes of superiority to those outside of their group, and consider themselves to be the definition of normal for everyone else.

Followers of Jesus live in the tension between separation from the world through their beliefs and practices of community, and connection with the world through daily life and just being human.

The value of salt is in its ability to enhance the flavor of its host. We can add the flavor of love, compassion and integrity to our host culture if we engage with it rather than isolate ourselves from it. In the process we need to remain salty ourselves or else we lose the *flavoring affect* on culture.

The light that we bring into the darkness of our culture is not just to expose it for what it is, but to enlighten it and reveal a different pathway. If a church is a subculture, it is hiding its light under a basket, when it should be shining its light on a hilltop.

One day, a young man in our church felt that God had told him to stand in the local park on the main road through town, holding a sign that said, "Free Prayer." Wanting to make sure it was God (Who else would ask him to do such a thing?), he asked Him to have the blank sign waiting for him in a dumpster at the next alley. Sure enough, there it was: an unused sign board and a lath stick to hold it. For months Guy spent his lunch-break standing in the park, praying for people, seeing them healed and become followers of Jesus. I think that was salt and light!

Church is a safe place for all people.

I was told this story by a pastor who had received a rather frantic telephone call from a fellow pastor. It was Valentine's Sunday and the church had a tradition of honoring couples for longevity in marriage, most children and the most recently married. The youth pastor was leading this part of the service. A lovely old couple stood to great applause as the longest married folks in the church. A young couple with several children stood to receive the gift for the largest family. And then, the unexpected happened. Two ladies stood to receive the newlywed gifts of roses and chocolates. They had been married the weekend before and were indeed the most recent marriage. There was a brief and somewhat awkward applause from a rather stunned and caught-off-guard crowd. The gifts were presented and the service continued. At the end of the service, with the pressure and insistence of the elders, the pastor retrieved the gifts from the ladies with an acknowledgement that they had made a mistake in presenting them. The next day the news media made this their headline story.

Far away in Hawaii the phone rang and the pastor pleaded for help to resolve this dilemma that was now a public outcry for justice. The pastor in Hawaii simply advised that being "real" and human and Christ-like was all that could be done. An apology needed to be made, an acknowledgement of making a mistake and being unprepared for something like this. What better place could there be for these two ladies than in a loving, caring family of followers of Jesus who could authentically love them as He does? The damage was done and the press enjoyed another opportunity to criticize the church for its bigotry and lack of love.

In the class I teach at Pacific Life Bible College, I conduct a forum on this story, allowing the students to represent the different groups involved. It is always interesting to watch them struggle with their preconceived ideas about the Gay community, with their religious bias towards rejecting anyone with a different sexual orientation than themselves, with their desire to be like Jesus, and their commitment to remain orthodox in their beliefs. They have come to recognize that the church seldom addresses the issue of multiple sexual partners among heterosexual men and women who attend the church, while proclaiming homosexuality as the worst of offenses against God. If it was on God's short list of sins, I have to believe that Jesus would have addressed it while living in a Roman culture that condoned it fully.

Please do not take the easy way out by accusing me of being liberal or unorthodox. I am neither! I am a follower of Jesus grappling with how I can be Jesus within the culture that I have been born. How can I express the love of God to people who are vastly different from me? How can I stop placing the sentence of death upon them by judging them before they have even met the Jesus that I proclaim? I cannot get the story of the adulterous woman brought to Jesus out of my mind (John 8:10). Her accusers were trying to trick Jesus into making a mistake in judgment by showing her leniency. Instead, they walked away under Godly conviction, apparently feeling guilty for their own shortcomings. The woman stood before the One who had every right to judge her, but she was confronted instead with the most authentic love in the universe. Even though men intended to condemn (damn) her, He did not. Jesus did not appear to categorize sins like we do, except that He seemed to hate the arrogance of the religious leaders. He saw people as special and unique and worthy of genuine love and acceptance and forgiveness. How can we do anything less than that?

Church is breaking bread together.

They (early Christians) followed a daily discipline of worship in the Temple followed by meals at home, every meal a celebration, exuberant and joyful, as they praised God. People in general liked what they saw. Acts 2:46-47 The Message

I heard Wolfgang Simson, author of **Houses That Change the World**, (1999, C&P Publishing, Emmelsbull, Germany) say that we need more "meating" times together, changing one "e" to "a" to coin a new word to incorporate eating into our meetings. Food is not only one of our basic physical needs, but can be a catalyst for our basic spiritual and psychological need for fellowship. Sharing a meal together in our home creates a wonderful opportunity for community to take place. Jesus modeled a pattern of eating with friends and sinners alike. Over the years, Ellie and I have served some very simple, inexpensive and unimpressive meals (by some standards) to provide a time and space for fellowship. It is less about the eating and more about the meeting.

Celebrating the Lord's Supper (communion) is another time for breaking bread together. Some of my most memorable times of celebrating communion took place outside the walls of a church building. We often ended a shared meal in our home with a simple, but deeply meaningful breaking of bread together. Our Emerge young leaders always responded with enthusiasm to simple, creative ways of remembering Christ's death and resurrection. These were highly spiritual times celebrated in the midst of real life. We gathered at one point in time in a large open room, sitting in a circle around a simple cross made from concrete blocks stacked on each other. Around the perimeter of the circle we had setup five different stations, each representing one of our senses. We played recorded music as everyone had the opportunity to visit each station. Each person had a folder to hold the individual inserts that were available at each station. We smelled a cloth soaked in frankincense and myrrh and then wrote about the grave clothes in Jesus' tomb and how death has affected us. After seeing an artist's drawing of a woman trapped in a large web, we wrote about the things that we need to find freedom from in our lives. Large rusty nails were felt to help us relate to the pain of the crucifixion and then write about the things that cause pain in us and through us to others. As we covered our ears with sound-proof ear protectors, we tried to imagine the sounds that were heard in the midst of the death and horror of Golgatha, and then write any new insights that we had about what Christ did for us there. Finally we tasted the bread and drank the grape juice in an intensely personal time of not only remembering His death, but celebrating the wonderful spiritual life that we were experiencing.

Communion should be a highlight of our times together, not just an add-on to an already busy order-of-service. There is so much spiritual benefit that can accompany this *Christ-*

originated celebration if we will re-discover its beauty and meaning.

Church is prayer.

I often felt guilty about missing a prayer meeting at church. Those times seemed to showcase the truly spiritual and those who had a better grasp of King James English than me. I think that conversations with God flowing from sincere hearts, without the use of formulas or "vain repetitions" is prayer. It is so important for the church to remain dependant upon the Head of the church, and one of the ways of expressing that dependence is through prayer.

I remember hearing Dr. C. Peter Wagner at Fuller Seminary saying that his personal "prayer life" was growing as a result of times spent with other followers who were sincerely seeking God for direction in their lives and interceding on behalf of many others. Corporate times of prayer remind us all of our own shortcomings and our need for God, while at the same time giving us opportunity to focus on the needs of others. This is community and mission combined in a spiritual exercise that connects directly to the Father.

Church is worship.

I sat yesterday in a building devoted to faith community gatherings and worshipped with my voice and heart and hands along with fellow followers and a "worship team" of gifted musicians. I also sat yesterday overlooking Hood Canal, watching a soaring eagle and a playful seal against the backdrop of glistening waters and deep-green foothills. I stood last night to view the beauty of a star-filled sky, the Milky Way flowing with its myriad of lights like a stream above my head, shooting stars chasing each other to both horizons. It all felt like worship!

A number of years ago I was teaching a series of sermons on worship. I had completed a portion of the teachings using several Hebrew words used to describe various facets of this fascinating subject. I thought that I had arrived at a pretty good understanding of what it was all about. Then, early one morning out behind the old barn on our property, I learned some more.

As I stood in the moist sandy soil overlooking the peach orchard, I became aware of hundreds of little birds that had perched on a high electrical line above me. They sat in silence. I thanked God for the beauty of the morning mist, the smells of ripening fruit and the company of His little creatures that had joined in on my devotions. I then heard a clear impression within my soul that was too strange for even me to have initiated it. I heard these words within me, "Lead the birds in worship!" My first thought was that I had wandered off in my mind and needed to get back to reality. But, the voice repeated the simple command. I wish I could tell you that I immediately and enthusiastically responded, but in fact I looked around very carefully to make sure that no farm-workers were in sight, and did a 360 search for anyone who might be about to witness my insanity. It was down to me and the birds.

They still sat in perfect silence. I raised my hands as if I was a symphony conductor calling the orchestra to order. When I began to move my arms as if calling the instruments to enter into the overture, an amazing thing happened. The birds all began to sing! When I stopped leading, they stopped singing. It was exhilarating and joyful and spontaneous and strangely normal. Nature itself was teaching me that worship is something that is so far beyond my ability to plan or facilitate that I need His creatures to remind me of its creative boundlessness. It is so much more than singing songs or hymns or even "spiritual songs" from my heart. It is a lifestyle that perceives the beauty and awesomeness of our

Creator. It is an appreciation of His insatiable desire to place objects of His own creativity before our eyes.

Ellie and I have been blessed to be able to develop friendships with so many young people who are gifted in the arts. We have heard the pain in their hearts as they have tried to incorporate who they are into a church culture that doesn't fully embrace the arts as a spiritual form of worship. The incredible beauty of Michelangelo's paintings on the ceiling of the Sistine Chapel in Rome remind us that expressions of an artist's heart are interlinked with faith and the pursuit of relationship with the Creator. The Emergent Church movement is rediscovering the diversity of expressions of worship that are resident in the hearts and souls of people, that need both the opportunity and the encouragement of church leaders to be set free. There will be new music, new paintings, new poetry, new dances, new films and videos and documentaries, new musical instruments, new theatre, and new writings. Churches that provide the time and space to artists to create new forms of worship will enhance the attempts of all its people to express their souls to God.

I discovered some wonderful thoughts about worship from ***The Prodigal Project …Journey into the Emerging Church.***

> *Life is neither the candle or the wick, but the burning.*
>
> *Even so is worship neither the gathering of the people present nor what they say or do, but the sharing of an experience of the presence of God, and a celebration of that experience.*
>
> *Good worship connects the lives of the worshippers with the life of God. "We're here to seek and be sought by God" is a fitting call to worship.*

Church is prophetic.

And of the sons of Issachar, men who understood the times, with knowledge of what Israel should do, 1 Chronicles 12:32 NAS

The church should be a prophetic voice within culture. The sons of Issachar had knowledge regarding the seasons in which they lived, with the important ability to discover and discern what to do with that knowledge.

Most of the prophetic function of the church has been turned inward. Like the proverbial traveling "medicine show" of the old western era, prophetic ministries have taken their spiritual "elixirs" on the road, touring the church circuit to guide the sheep into new pastures, while collecting substantial fees for their wares. There has been such a demand for "seers" to tell me about my future and to make the discovery of God's will somehow easier for me, that the gift has too often surpassed the spiritual character of the prophet. The Gifts of the Spirit have been given by Christ to the church to do His works. The Fruit of the Spirit give us the opportunity to become more like Jesus in character. We have witnessed too much gift and too little fruit.

Is the purpose of the prophetic primarily to call people out of a gathering to "read their mail" in public? Is it given to showcase certain special individuals in the church who gather followers from far and wide to come to their meetings in hope of being selected to receive a "word"? Does superstar ministry in any way reflect what Jesus modeled?

Paul wrote in 1 Corinthians chapter 14 that the primary purpose for the prophetic is "edification and exhortation and consolation". This does not appear to be limited to a church context, but should be the normal function of the prophetic gift wherever one finds themselves. If I am in line at the grocery checkout and I am prophetic, I will speak words of comfort into the broken soul of a cashier who has just suffered loss. I will build people up and encourage them.

We have somehow been led to believe that spiritual gifts are to be primarily consumed by the church to make us happier and healthier people. The problem is that we have missed many incredible opportunities to minister in the marketplace with the spiritual insight and power that only comes from Christ's gifts. The church is gifted so that we can be truly missional within a culture that desperately needs gifts of healing and miracles, discerning of spirits, words of wisdom and knowledge, and faith for impossible situations. If we are prophetic people we will understand the times and have knowledge of what we are to do in these times.

Church is favorable.

We read in Acts 2:42 that the early church had "favor with all the people". This favor did not come from compromising with the culture, but from being people of integrity, living lives consistent with the faith that they preached.

I have witnessed so many events that have turned my culture against the church because of inconsistency and bigotry. We cannot hope to be seen as favorable if we refuse to live lifestyles that mirror the message of our faith. My daughter, Sarah, gave me a fridge magnet for Christmas that pretty much sums up the attitude of some in my culture. It reads: "JESUS IS COOL but some of His followers give me the creeps."

I am reminded of a conversation that Tony Campolo had with a university president about the apparent rejection of evangelicals on that campus. The president's response was that even the most radical groups on campus would tell Tony that they admire Jesus and what He stands for, but Christians were not anything like the Jesus of the Bible. This is so painful to hear, but it is important for us to know how we are perceived by people that Jesus wants us to love.

Church is incarnational.

The Word became flesh and blood, and moved into the neighborhood. We saw the glory with our own eyes, the one-of-a-kind glory, like Father, like Son, Generous inside and out, true from start to finish. John1:14 The Message

Historically the church has functioned as an "attractional" enterprise requiring those whom we would desire to influence to leave their own "secular" context and enter into our "sacred" context to receive something of our "sacredness." Our buildings, programs, musicians, drama teams, coffee and donuts and sermons all combine to create an attraction to be attended. One of my favorite movies was Field of Dreams with the famous line, If you build it they will come! We may not be building a baseball diamond in the mid-western town of Dyersville, Iowa, but we have "cathedralized" our mission by building places and programs that we hope will result in them coming to us. Was it ever Jesus' intention that non-Christians should seek us out and desire to come to our worship event at our church location? The idea of incarnational ministry is to follow the example of Jesus by becoming "fleshed-out" in the world, not sequestered in the cathedral. Even the language that we use in our context can be foreign to the outsider.

In ***Amazing Grace: A Vocabulary of Faith***, (1998, Riverhead Books, New York, NY 10014) in her chapter God-Talk, Kathleen Norris writes:

When God-talk is speech that is not of this world, it is a false language. In a religion that celebrates

> the Incarnation... the joining together of the human and the divine... a spiritualized jargon that does not ground itself in the five senses should be anathema. But the human tendency to disincarnate language is a strong one. But when a sermon is little but biblical or theological terminology that the preacher has not troubled to digest, to incarnate, as it were, so that it might readily translate into the lives of (his people), it is often worse than no sermon at all. The preacher has not done what I consider the real work of writing, and if the sermon is so full of God-talk as to lack a recognizably human voice, the presence of a person behind it all, why should other people be troubled to listen to it?

Incarnational ministry is practicing one's faith **with** others, not "to" or "for" others. If I seek to be engaged with people who are on the margins of our society, I must first seek to listen to and be grounded in the inner city context. How can I possibly be identified as part of their context if I am unwilling to be with them? I earn the right to engage them in conversations of spirituality by coming in humility, rather than with arrogant evangelism birthed in a superior view of myself and my faith. I must know their context, must listen carefully to those who live in it, and then, develop models of ministry with those who live in that context. This kind of ministry requires long-term involvement with the people and in the places that the church usually ignores or verbally judges from a distance. I must earn the right to speak in that context!

Ultimately, incarnational ministry is about friendship, about unconditional love. Jesus' choice to be a friend of sinners did not win Him points with the religious elite, and we should expect the same. I recently heard Pastor Deborah Loyd of The Bridge in Portland, Oregon say that if you want to connect with people in culture, you should go to their parties. That would be quite a stretch for some of us evangelicals, wouldn't it? But then again there was Jesus!

I remember the impact of the few words written above the doorway of Church On The Way in Van Nuys, California. Jack Hayford wanted his people to understand the meaning of the church context. When you entered from the outside it read: You are entering the Living Room. This was the place for the family to gather to be fed and nurtured, a place of support and preparation. When you turned to leave, the words above the exit read: You are entering the Mission Field. This was a constant reminder of incarnating the good news into real life outside the doors of the church building. It defined the mission of every believer in terms of a context "out there" not "in here."

In 1962, Don Richardson and his wife Carol, embarked on a mission to the cannibalistic head-hunters of New Guinea. He wrote of his experiences in the book ***Peace Child*** (2003, YWAM Publishing, Seattle, WA 98155). In his introduction Don writes:

> *The key God gave us to the heart of the Sawi people was the principle of redemptive analogy – the application to local custom of spiritual truth. The principle we discerned was that God had already provided for the evangelization of these people by means of redemptive analogies in their own culture. These analogies were our stepping stones, the secret entryway by which the gospel came into the Sawi culture and started both a spiritual and a social revolution from within.*
>
> *As Carol and I ministered to the Sawi by means of the "peace child" and other redemptive analogies, we watched in suspense to see if the Spirit of God would actually use this means of communication for*

the regeneration of these cannibalistic, head-hunting people. He did!

This story is an exceptional example of incarnational ministry. If you have not read it, I highly recommend it.

It might be good to point out that Jesus, through His teaching and miracles certainly attracted large crowds of seekers. The attraction was not primarily programmatic, but rather centered in prophetic teaching that pierced the hearts of the listeners, and signs and wonders that pointed them to a powerful, yet lovingly personal God who cared about their diseases and pain. Perhaps the opposite of incarnational ministry is the "canned" variety that depends on formulas and vain repetitions for its success.

Incarnational ministers identify with the pain and suffering of those to whom they minister, and empty themselves of the thoughts and things that cause them to have a condescending attitude. They actively share in the life of the crowd, with its fears, frustrations and afflictions, employing the language and thought forms of those to whom they seek to share the good news. They do not take God out of the human situation, in fact they look for His already being involved at every turn. This kind of minister is at risk of failure and is vulnerable to the deep pain that accompanies loving much. They go to where the people are, not expecting them to come to their places. They communicate the gospel by many ordinary means like acts of serving, relationship building and good deeds. They earn the right to share their words of truth by living lives that model the incarnation of that same truth.

South American theologians use the term "integral"; North Americans prefer "holistic"; all defining incarnational ministry. The emphasis is upon using both words and deeds in our witness to the world. Historically there has been a split between the liberal "social gospel" and the conservative "verbal gospel" approaches to witness. Liberals have been accused of offering social justice without proclaiming the gospel. Conservatives have been accused of proclamation without seeking social change or justice. Neither view adequately responds to the idea that God's kingdom is **both** *present* (to bring about social change and justice here and now) and future (living in eternal connection with God because of conversion here). The real issue here is whether or not proclaimed truth without accompanying deeds and lifestyles that reflect God's kingdom is the true gospel.

Church is missional.

Think of yourselves the way Christ Jesus thought of himself: He had equal status with God but didn't think so much of himself that he had to cling to the advantages of that status no matter what: Not at all. When the time came, he set aside the privileges of deity and took on the status of a slave, became human! Having become human, he stayed human. It was an incredibly humbling process. He didn't claim special privileges. Instead, he lived a selfless, obedient life and then died a selfless, obedient death – and the worst kind of death at that: a crucifixion. Philippians 2:6-8, The Message

The Bible is a missionary book whose primary character is a missionary God who desires to raise up a missionary people. Mission begins with God: a personal being who seeks lost and alienated humanity. His story is filled with His longing to reconnect with people that He loves and misses. If mission is part of the nature of God, then to be committed to this God must also mean to be committed to mission. Mission then, is not a human idea, but a God idea! The mission of God is seen clearly in the incarnation of Jesus who had a mindset of selfless giving to others regardless of personal sacrifice.

A ***Relevantmagazine.com*** article said the following:

> "Incarnation" is a funky word. It means the act of giving bodily form and substance to something that is unseen. We don't use it much unless we're talking theology, but we need to get it back into our vocabulary. In the last 50 years the western church has fallen into a very, very bad pattern of "mission's professionalism." It is the philosophy that missions is best left to highly trained, highly called, special-force type Christians who will go out there and save the world. For the rest of us, our role is to stay home, send money, stick magnetic prayer cards on our refrigerators and listen to Sara Groves sing about her missionary grandma. We think that unless we have a seminary education and hear the audible voce of God telling us to go that we should stay put. Of course, this idea is completely ridiculous.
>
> When Jesus said, "Go and make disciples of all nations" he was speaking to an unsophisticated, rag-tag group. He was calling them to incarnational ministry. <u>He wanted them to make disciples in the</u> name of the Father, Son and Holy Spirit and to give, through their (unsophisticated, but Spirit-filled) presence, substance to the triune God who is invisible but real. He didn't tell them to merely send people to the nations; he told them to <u>go personally</u> to the nations. And they did! In describing the first disciples, Justin Martyr said: "They were uneducated and of no ability in speaking. But by the power of God, they proclaimed to every race of men that they were sent by Christ to teach the word of God to everyone". Two centuries later, the early church still knew nothing

of mission's professionals. About 197 A.D. Tertullian wrote, "We are but of yesterday, and we have filled every place among you – cities, islands, fortresses, towns, marketplaces, senate, forum – we have left nothing to you but the temples of your gods." It seems like everybody in the early church was explosively focused on missions.

In his book, ***Ancient-Future Evangelism*** (2003, Baker Books, Grand Rapids, MI) Robert Webber defines missional church in very clear language:

The missional church rejects the association of Christianity with American values and the association of the church with entertainment, marketing, and corporate business models. The missional church is reading both Scripture and culture with new eyes. It sees that what is determined by the Christian faith is more than being a good, upright citizen. It sees the church as something different from the smooth corporate model of business. This emerging church calls for honest, authentic faith that seeks to be church in the way of a more radical discipleship. (129)

An important component in the missional church is an understanding that we "are" the church before we "do" church, our mission precedes our meetings. Jesus is recorded in John 20:21 as saying, "As the Father has sent me, I am sending you." This means that our being sent by Him is the very foundation of our "doing" church. For someone like me who has taught the ecclesiology (study of the church) course at a Christian college for several years, this has been a very important understanding. Our missiology (understanding of our mission) must precede our ecclesiology. One of the implications of this is that we must build missional relationships before we make plans for how we will do church. If our mission is primary, then we will think differently about how we see ourselves as church. I am being stretched by understanding what Jesus meant, but as I regain perspective on God's mission through Christ, I can begin to understand the mission on which He has sent me.

Let me try to describe a missional church. It is focused outward rather than inward, so that the Sunday gathering is not seen as the main event. It is engaging with the culture around it without being absorbed by that culture. Being incarnational is always valued above being institutional. Discipling others, whether they attend church events or not, is far more important than church membership. They align themselves with God's missionary purpose in the world, seeking to establish new places where God rules in the hearts of people. Multiplying other communities with the same missionary focus is their goal. New leaders are trained and equipped by participating in the mission, not staying in the classroom. Character and compassion expressed in deeds of kindness are seen as a strong and effective witness. They are connected to Jesus more through the commonality of mission with Him, than through being doctrinally precise about Him. Organizational structure and forms exist and function for the sake of mission rather than to fulfill some obligation to denominational tradition. It is organic in nature, ready and willing to grow and change to fulfill its calling. Relationships are developed that cross the lines of generations, ethnicity, economics and cultures. They walk alongside their community to partner with them to seek the blessing of peace upon all of its inhabitants. Times of assembling together are for seeking God and further understanding His missionary purpose. A missional church sees broken communities as invitations to enter not warnings to avoid. Being missional cannot be something that we try to add onto our already over-busy lives, but must instead be a part of our real life as it is right now, being Jesus right where we are!

We become the missional presence of Jesus wherever we are by the way we live (presence of Jesus) and what we do (behavior of Jesus). The church cannot simply run a business of selling religious goods and services to consumers. We must be about the work of God's kingdom and understand the church in the framework of that kingdom. The kingdom is the place of the rule and reign of God-activity, and we participate with Him to engage culture with the amazing good news that the kingdom is here through the gospel of Jesus, and we demonstrate its affect by our own lives and lifestyles. It is, after all, my present life that the gospel has to make sense of, not just give me a future hope of something meaningful after I die. In Mark 1:14-15 we read that Jesus came into Galilee preaching the gospel of God. He said, "The time is fulfilled, and the kingdom of God is at hand; repent and believe in the gospel". A timeframe was fulfilled and the kingdom had arrived; this was the gospel of Jesus. In 1 Corinthians 15:3-6 we read the gospel about Jesus. The message there is that Jesus lived, Jesus died and was buried, Jesus rose again, and Jesus appeared to many and commissioned them and us to preach this gospel.

To be missional is based in understanding God's own heart for mission and then in partnering with Him in the wonderful things He is already doing! In 2004, the Lausanne Conference on World Evangelization defined missional churches as *"those communities of Christ-followers who see the church as the people of God who are sent on a mission."*

There is movement away from church being a club for Christians, towards church being sent by God into the world as reconcilers. To be missional also becomes every believers' involvement in God's purposes as opposed to a few "good women and men" being sent out on mission's activities in some representative capacity for the rest of us. Words like "missions" and "missionary" carry so much baggage from the past that new words and new revelation need to surface. In reality, because we are rethinking the role of the church within our own culture, we are redefining our ecclesiology (study of the church) as much as our missiology (study of missions). I find myself returning to my lifelong question: What is the church?

In his book, **The Present Future** (2003, Jossey-Bass, San Francisco, CA 94103) Reggie McNeal encourages us to ask some searching questions in the process of moving towards becoming missional churches.

The collapse of church culture:
Wrong question: How do we do church better?
Tough question: How do we reconvert from "churchianity" to Christianity?

The shift from church growth to kingdom growth:
Wrong question: How do we grow this church?
Tough question: How do we transform our community?

A new reformation: Releasing God's people:
Wrong question: How do we turn members into ministers?
Tough question: How do we turn members into missionaries?

The return to spiritual formation:
Wrong question: How do we develop church members?
Tough question: How do we develop followers of Jesus?

The shift from planning to preparation:
Wrong question: How do we plan for the future?
Tough question: How do we prepare for the future?

The rise of apostolic leadership:
Wrong question: How do we develop leaders for church work?
Tough question: How do we develop leaders for the Christian movement?

Church is socially just.

> He has told you, O man, what is good; and what does the LORD require of you, but to do justice, to love kindness, and to walk humbly with your God? Micah 6:8 NAS
>
> I was hungry and you fed me, I was thirsty and you gave me a drink, I was homeless and you gave me a room, I was shivering and you gave me clothes, I was sick and you stopped to visit, I was in prison and you came to me. Whenever you did one of these things to someone overlooked or ignored, that was me – you did it to me. Matthew 25:35,36,40 The Message

I was reminded recently of the amazing legacy of William and Catherine Booth, founders of the Salvation Army. At the age of 13, William was sent to work in a pawnbroker's shop to help support his mother and sisters. This unfulfilling job gave him insight into the humiliation of the poor as they pawned whatever they could to try to keep alive. He later became a Methodist minister, preaching to the poor in London's East End. It was there that he developed strong views on the role of church ministers, that they should be "loosing the chains of injustice, freeing the captive and oppressed, sharing food and home, clothing the naked, and carrying out family responsibilities." This sounds vaguely familiar doesn't it! He formed his own organization called "The Christian Mission", which eventually became The Salvation Army. He once proclaimed:

> *While women weep, as they do now, I'll fight; while children go hungry, as they do now I'll fight; while men go to prison, in and out, in and out, as they do now, I'll fight; while there is a drunkard left, while there is a poor lost girl upon the streets, while there remains one dark soul without the light of God, I'll fight, I'll fight to the very end!*

He was devoted to a balanced ministry of preaching and practice, not willing to separate one from the other. The following quotes give us some understanding of his own struggle to keep the two in tension:

> *To get a man soundly saved it is not enough to put on him a pair of new breeches, to give him regular work, or even to give him a University education. These things are all outside a man, and if the inside remains unchanged you have wasted your labor. You must in some way or other graft upon the man's nature a new nature, which has in it the element of the Divine.*
>
> *But what is the use of preaching the Gospel to men whose whole attention is concentrated upon a mad, desperate struggle to keep themselves alive?*

William was strongly influenced by his wife Catherine, who believed in equality for women, and that it was inadequate education and social customs that made them appear as men's intellectual inferiors. The Salvation Army gave women equal responsibility with men for preaching and the work of welfare. On one occasion William said that "My best men are women!" The Army was criticized by the Church of England for their "elevation of women to men's status."

The Booths were very actively involved in improving the working conditions for women. The Bryant and May match factory paid measly wages for 16 hour days working with toxic yellow phosphorus that left many of them sick and caused some to die. When Booth pointed out to the company that harmless red phosphorus was used by the rest of Europe, they countered that it would be too expensive for them to change. In 1891 The Army opened its own match factory using red phosphorus and paying women twice what Bryant and May were paying.

They also cared for multitudes of street waifs, feeding and clothing them and educating them in the basics that could improve their future state.

Over the past several years, the involvement of most evangelicals in social or justice issues has sadly degenerated to only two: abortion and homosexuality. The recent death of Jerry Falwell brought renewed coverage of this Moral Majority agenda. Regardless of how passionate you are about these two issues, it is obvious that global poverty, abuse of women and children, war and its accompanying crimes, human trafficking by the international sex trade, need for safe drinking water, greed of multi-national corporations, health care, the AIDS crisis, immigration, the unquestioning patriotism of Americanized Christianity, and any issue that creates marginalized peoples have been almost unaddressed by the church. It seems to me that justice in the Bible is about healing the brokenness in all relationships, loving all who are created in the image of God, going about doing good.

Biblical justice can be stated much more fully in terms of what we are "for" rather than what we are against. I read once that Mother Teresa was asked if she would join a rally to march against some injustice. She replied that she never marched "against" anything but would join them if they marched "for" something instead. My concern for the church is that we are known primarily for what we are against, rather than what we are for, and this alienates from us the very people who desperately seek authentic love.

I was one of those who detested and verbally bashed homosexuals, until I met a number of wonderful young men and women who were either fully involved or fully struggling with their homosexual identity. They were no different from me in their desire to have a sense of hope and future, to be loved unconditionally as human beings, to be valued and accepted. I was one who protested against abortion, but I have been humbled by the stories of women who at the point of their greatest need to be embraced and received, have been abused and rejected by the church that calls itself by Christ's name. I am "for" the healing of broken people regardless of the source of their brokenness.

Compassion can be practiced anywhere at anytime: on the beach, in a store, at the airport, in a church building, whenever we are together with other people. One of the ways of learning to focus on others is to begin to see them through different eyes. How can I see them? I can see them like I see myself. They desire happiness in their lives. I see them trying to avoid pain or dealing with current issues that have caused pain. I see them as people who have been shaped by sadness or loneliness or loss. I see them as people who have had dreams and hopes for themselves and their family which they may still have or may have abandoned because of circumstances. I see them in the process of learning about life. I see them as created in God's image, deeply loved by Him, being pursued by His love even as our lives intersect for even a brief moment in time. Compassion is not a feeling that I must somehow create within myself to then use in a condescending approach to those perceived less than myself.

It is instead treating others as I wish to be treated myself. That too sounds familiar!

Bob Rowland said it well when he wrote his prose **Listen Everybody:**

> *I was hungry and you formed a humanities club and discussed my hunger.*
> *I was imprisoned and you crept off quietly to your chapel in the cellar and prayed for my release.*
> *I was naked and in your mind you debated the morality of my appearance.*
> *I was sick and you thanked God for your health.*
> *I was homeless and you preached to me of the spiritual shelter of the love of God.*
> *I was lonely and you left me alone to pray for me.*
> *You seem so holy; so close to God.*
> *But I'm still very hungry,*
> *And lonely,*
> *And cold.*

Church is transformational.

When all else is said, the essence of church is changed people and cultures and nations. The good news of the gospel is centered upon a transformation from an old way of living to a new life, an old way of thinking to a renewed mind, old selfishness to selfless servant-hood, and old religious formulas to new intimate relationship with God.

Church is people in love with Jesus, forgiven by God, filled with the Holy Spirit, going about doing good and telling others through their words and deeds how they too can be transformed.

PART FOUR: Next Rest Stop 50 Miles!

It's really not over until it's over!
Progress assumes that no permanent stopping place has been adopted.
DH

In three words I can sum up everything I've learned about life:
It goes on.
Robert Frost

Time is a dressmaker specializing in alterations.
Faith Baldwin

Wisdom begins at the end.
Daniel Webster

TWENTY-ONE:

On the Road Again!

*Behold, I will do something new,
Now it will spring forth;
Will you not be aware of it?*
Isaiah 43:19 NASB

*There are times in our lives
when we must walk away from
the familiar, the comfortable, the recognizable.*
DH

The theme song of our wanderings, "On the Road Again" was revived a few weeks ago when we packed our final load of earthly goods into our van and homemade trailer. I have heard it said that the three most emotionally traumatic events in our lives are death, divorce and moving. We have experienced the process of dealing with grief on too many occasions, have never personally walked through divorce (for which we are very grateful), but we have become somewhat connoisseurs of the moving elite. Keeping in mind the wonderfully encouraging quote from JRR Tolkien, "Not all those who wander are lost," we again joined the ranks of the mobile and headed for Shoreline, Washington.

On Valentine's Day as we were waiting for our name to be called for dinner at Red Lobster, I was reflecting on those final moments of scouring the Cloverdale house for treasures left in secret corners of cupboards and shelves. The trailer and van were literally overflowing with the fruit of our lives and I was exhausted from the previous days of sorting, packing, thinning, selling and tossing. As I stood at the back door and took one final look into what had been our "peaceful habitation" for the past seven years, I felt the sadness that comes from leaving the familiar behind along with the joyfulness of the many wonderful relationships that began and grew in that place. The anxiety that attaches itself to many unanswered questions in our lives was certainly drifting in and out of my thoughts.

There in the corner of the dining room, half hidden by unused boxes and packing paper, sat my old leather slippers. I had worn them daily while calling this place home. There was a hole in the left slipper where the leather lacing had broken and my big toe had found its freedom. The right slipper was badly stained in a sort of grayish color as proof that it had witnessed the winter's repainting of my motorcycle gas tank. I reached down to retrieve these treasured friends. As if my hands were held back by some other force than my own will, I stopped reaching for them, turned and walked away, leaving them sitting in their quiet corner.

At Red Lobster I began to understand the meaning of the abandoned slippers. They had been new at one point in time and needed to be broken in to fit my feet and my way of walking. Over time they had become very comfortable, easy to slip into. Yet, in recent days my feet were often cold even with extra socks due to the worn-out lining, the hole and the unstitched parts. Even though they still fit, they were discolored and soiled from much use.

In Search of the Church

There are times in our lives when we must walk away from the familiar, the comfortable, the recognizable. Our journey leads from the known into the unknown. If we cannot leave the *old slippers* behind, we may miss the beauty, the warmth and the fresh 'fit' of the new pair that awaits us. Slippers have a useful lifespan. When their fullness of time has come, we must leave them behind.

As I write today, I am enjoying the warmth and comfort of the nicest, warmest (Australian Sheep's' wool-lined) pair of slippers that I have ever placed on my feet. God delights in doing new things in us and through our uniqueness. We must remain willing to discard our old ways and embrace His new ways without missing the lessons He has been teaching us. His new things are most often a return with new understanding to His ancient things.

I stood on the pier at the edge of Lake Washington last night and watched a mother Mallard Duck with her troop of three little ducklings. Her kids had a mind of their own and swam in different directions snapping at passing mosquitoes and slurping up an occasional piece of drifting grass. When she realized that a large mammal (me) was looking down upon her family, she began to corral the little ones with a series of swimming maneuvers. In a very short period of time, she had all of them lined up in a perfect formation heading off to the safety of the nest. Many times I have tried to "get my ducks in a row", to have the kind of control that leads to a life of predictable direction. The story of the feedlot filled with *bovine butts* in Washington still reminds me of my daily need to follow God with my whole heart as well as my mind and strength.

Transitions come from different sources: death of a friend or family member, developers level your home to build a new hotel, doors close to opportunity that seems to match your gifts and passion, God does something new somewhere else and you want to be in the middle of it, you get too old to

209

be a youth pastor anymore, or you've just worked yourself out of a job because you were such a good mentor.

My hope for you is that you will continue to search for what is true, both about yourself and about the church. If God delights in doing new things, may we never settle for the way we've always done it. Perhaps the yearning that you feel deep within your heart is a fresh stirring from God. What will it mean for you? What does Jesus intend His church to be today? Let's discover it together.

May your journey be blessed!

"Organism" 149 170
Christian A Schwarz Survey... 175 stars⁸

169 theme?   171 ent heart mystery
164 relevance   (to Know + Be Known)
160 teaching   161 types of evangelism

       121 Stress — prevention
115 authentic — reason for writing

78, 79   Inward Upward Outward
           trowels swords   Wagon wheel
           Building Battling   hub rim spokes

         pain
35   74   109   111   112   115   116
     hostile   117 healing through sharing
        71
painful 172/

Printed in the United States
134252LV00004B/1/A